D0989761

The Usborne
World of
Animals

Susanna Davidson and Mike Unwin

Designed by

Andrea Slane and Michelle Lawrence

Additional designs by Catherine Mackinnon

Digital designer: John Russell

Illustrated by Lee Montgomery and Ian Jackson

Consultants: Dr. Margaret Rostron and Dr. John Rostron

Contents

Internet links

Throughout this book we have recommended websites where you can find out more about animals and watch video clips, play games and test your knowledge with interactive quizzes. To visit the sites, go to the Usborne Quicklinks Website at **www.usborne-quicklinks.com** and enter the keywords: world of animals.

How to use Usborne Quicklinks

Tundra and taiga

South of the Arctic Ocean lies a windswept stretch of land known as tundra. It is too cold for trees to grow there and the soil stays frozen all year round. South of the tundra lies the taiga, the largest band of forest in the world, home to bears, deer and countless small mammals and birds.

Surviving winter

Most animals leave the tundra during winter. The ones that remain are extremely hardy. Mice and lemmings keep warm by spending the winter in burrows under the snow, feeding on hay and seeds they have collected over the summer. Snowshoe hares spend the winter above ground. Their thick fur keeps them warm – it covers their entire bodies, even the gaps between their toes. They search for food on well-established trails, which become deeply worn in the snow.

This snowshoe hare's large back feet help to keep it from sinking into the snow.

98

This is a herd of male wapiti on the edge of the taiga. They have long, spindly legs to help them trek through the deep snow.

Chewing antlers

Many deer species, including moose, caribou and wapiti, live in the taiga. In winter, when food is scarce, they survive by eating bark and twigs. Then, late in winter, they shed their antlers. Deer sometimes chew on their old antlers to gain the extra minerals their bodies need.

> **Internet link**
> For a link to a website with a short video about life on the Arctic tundra, go to www.usborne-quicklinks.com

Changing coats

Tundra predators have to work hard to get their food. In winter, Arctic foxes follow polar bears to scavenge the remains of their kills, while stoats track prey by their scent over great distances. Both animals can change their coats to match the seasons, which helps to camouflage them as they hunt.

The Arctic fox's white winter coat makes it hard to see against the snow.

A stoat's coat during the summer

A stoat's coat during the winter

99

1. Look for the "Internet link" boxes throughout this book. They contain descriptions of the websites you can visit.
2. In your computer's web browser, type the address **www.usborne-quicklinks.com**
3. At the Usborne Quicklinks Website, type the keywords for this book: world of animals.
4. Type the page number of the link you want to visit. When the link appears, click on it to go to the recommended site.
The links in Usborne Quicklinks are regularly updated, but occasionally you may find a site is unavailable. This may only be temporary, so try again later.

> **Internet link**
> For a link to a website with a short video about life on the Arctic tundra, go to **www.usborne-quicklinks.com**

Pictures in this book marked with a ★ symbol can be downloaded from **www.usborne-quicklinks.com** for your own personal use. To download a picture, go to the website and follow the instructions there.

Net Help

For information and help using the Internet, go to the Net Help area on the Usborne Quicklinks Website. You'll find information about "plug-ins" – small free programs that your web browser needs to play videos, animations and sounds. You probably already have these, but if not, you can download them for free from Quicklinks Net Help. You can also find information about computer viruses and advice on anti-virus software to protect your computer.

What you'll find

Here are some examples of the many things you can do on the websites recommended in this book:

- listen to birds singing

- play a game matching heads, bodies and legs to create the correct animals

- watch video clips of baby animals

- take a photo safari to see African animals

- do a quiz to see how much you know about Australian animals

- go on a virtual exploration of the bottom of the ocean

Staying safe online

Make sure you follow these simple rules to keep you safe online:

You should ask an adult's permission before connecting to the Internet.

Never give out personal information about yourself, such as your real name, address, phone number or school.

If a site asks you to log in or register by typing your name and address, you should ask permission from an adult first.

If you receive an email from someone you don't know, don't reply to it. Tell an adult.

Notes for adults – the websites described in this book are regularly reviewed and updated, but websites can change and Usborne Publishing is not responsible for any site other than its own. We recommend that children are supervised while on the Internet, that they do not use Internet chat rooms and that filtering software is used to block unsuitable material.

Animal planet

Earth is the only known planet to support living things – and it teems with life. Animals are everywhere, from the top of the highest mountain to the bottom of the deepest ocean.

Animals are even found in Antarctica, the coldest place on Earth. These Adélie penguins are lining up to dive into the ice-cold Southern Ocean, which surrounds Antarctica.

Who lives where?

Some kinds, or species, of animals can flourish in almost any environment. Wolves are found in the ice-cold Arctic and in hot deserts, thick forests and open grasslands. Other animal species are much less widespread because they can only survive in one kind of environment. Giant pandas, for example, are only found in bamboo forests in China.

This Bengal tiger is splashing through water. Bengal tigers can only survive in dense bush or forests. They are also usually found near water, as they prey on animals that come to the water to drink.

New discoveries

Scientists are continually finding new animal species. One of the most spectacular discoveries was in 1977, when scientists found creatures living in total darkness around cracks in the ocean floor. Despite poisonous gases and boiling water spilling out of the cracks, species of shrimp and clam survive there, as well as worm-like animals called beardworms.

Internet link
For a link to a website packed with animal photographs, video clips and fun facts, go to **www.usborne-quicklinks.com**

This shows the animals that live around cracks in the ocean floor. The black cloud is made up of boiling water and minerals. The minerals provide food for bacteria, which are in turn fed on by shrimps, clams and beardworms.

Tropical haven

Animals are not distributed evenly across the Earth. The warm, wet conditions of rainforests make them the richest source of animal life in the world. Rainforests only cover 6% of the Earth's surface, but they contain over 50% of its animal species.

Amazing animals

Animals can do many mind-blowingly amazing things. There are fish that can leap out of rivers and glide through the air, insects that can jump up to 200 times their own length and birds that fly across the world and back each year. Scientists are still finding new ways of studying animals and exploring different areas on Earth, so there are many more amazing animal discoveries still to be made.

★
Large and small mammals, as well as countless insects, feed on vegetation or other animals on the forest floor.

★
Rainforest tree tops are home to birds and butterflies, as well as climbing animals, such as monkeys and tree anteaters.

This is a basilisk lizard. Its light weight, large feet and speed make it the only lizard in the world that can run on water.

The animal kingdom

There are millions of species of animals, from microscopic mites and giant blue whales to scaly sea snakes and slimy frogs. To make sense of this enormous variety, scientists divide all living creatures into groups.

Hairy animals

Human beings are just one of the thousands of species of mammals. Nearly all mammals give birth to live babies and feed them milk from their mammary glands, which is how mammals get their name. Most mammals are covered in hair or fur. This helps to keep them warm.

Internet link

For a link to a website where you can try putting animals into their correct groups, go to **www.usborne-quicklinks.com**

Dry and scaly

Snakes, crocodiles, lizards and turtles are all reptiles. Some reptiles give birth to live young, but most lay eggs. Reptiles have dry, scaly skin and are "cold-blooded" – meaning they do not have a constant body temperature. In order to survive, they have to keep moving between sun and shade.

A baby gibbon perches on its mother's shoulders as she swings through the trees. Like most baby mammals, it will be cared for by its mother until it is old enough to survive on its own.

A lizard basks in the morning sun to warm up.

It cools down during the hottest part of the day by hiding in the shade.

Feathers and eggs

Birds are the only animals that have feathers. All birds have wings too, but not all birds can fly. They lay eggs, usually in nests built in trees or on the ground. Birds would be too heavy to fly if they carried their babies around inside them.

These flycatcher chicks have opened their mouths to ask their mother for food.

Bug groups

The creatures most people describe as "bugs" are land animals that belong to a group called arthropods. They make up four-fifths of all known animal species. All bugs have a tough outer covering and six or more legs. You can tell different bugs apart by counting their legs.

This picture shows how scientists divide arthropods into smaller groups, according to the number of legs they have. True bugs and insects are shown together, as true bugs are a kind of insect.

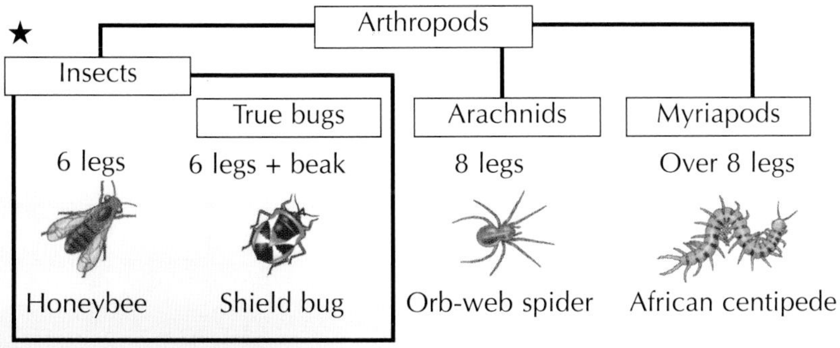

★

Arthropods			
Insects		**Arachnids**	**Myriapods**
	True bugs		
6 legs	6 legs + beak	8 legs	Over 8 legs
Honeybee	Shield bug	Orb-web spider	African centipede

Watery world

A huge variety of animals spend their lives in water, from fish, lobsters and jellyfish to mammals such as sea lions and dolphins. Some animals, known as amphibians, live both in and out of water. They include frogs, toads and newts.

This is an oriental fire-bellied toad. It lives in water in spring and summer, but buries itself in soft earth during winter.

On the move

From the fast-paced cheetah's bounding strides to the slow crawl of the caterpillar, animals move in many different ways. Some may seem better at it than others, but each animal moves according to its needs.

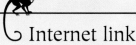

Internet link
For a link to a website where you can discover just how difficult it is to photograph flying frogs, go to **www.usborne-quicklinks.com**

This tree frog is using its giant webbed feet to glide through the air. Tree frogs can leap up to 15m (50ft) between trees.

Tree gliding

Some tree-dwelling animals, including certain species of frogs, lizards and squirrels, have flaps of skin between their limbs or toes. These enable them to glide from tree to tree. When they jump, they stretch out the flaps of skin like a parachute to slow down their fall.

Legging it

Animals use their legs in different ways. Most two-legged animals, such as kangaroos, bounce around on two legs at once, although some move one leg forward at a time. Four-legged animals usually walk by moving diagonally opposite legs together (for example, front left and back right). Many-legged animals, such as millipedes, begin by moving their back legs and finish by moving their front legs. Their legs appear to ripple in waves as they move.

These are impalas. They are fast-moving animals that run by stretching out their front and back legs, then bringing them together to make powerful bounding movements.

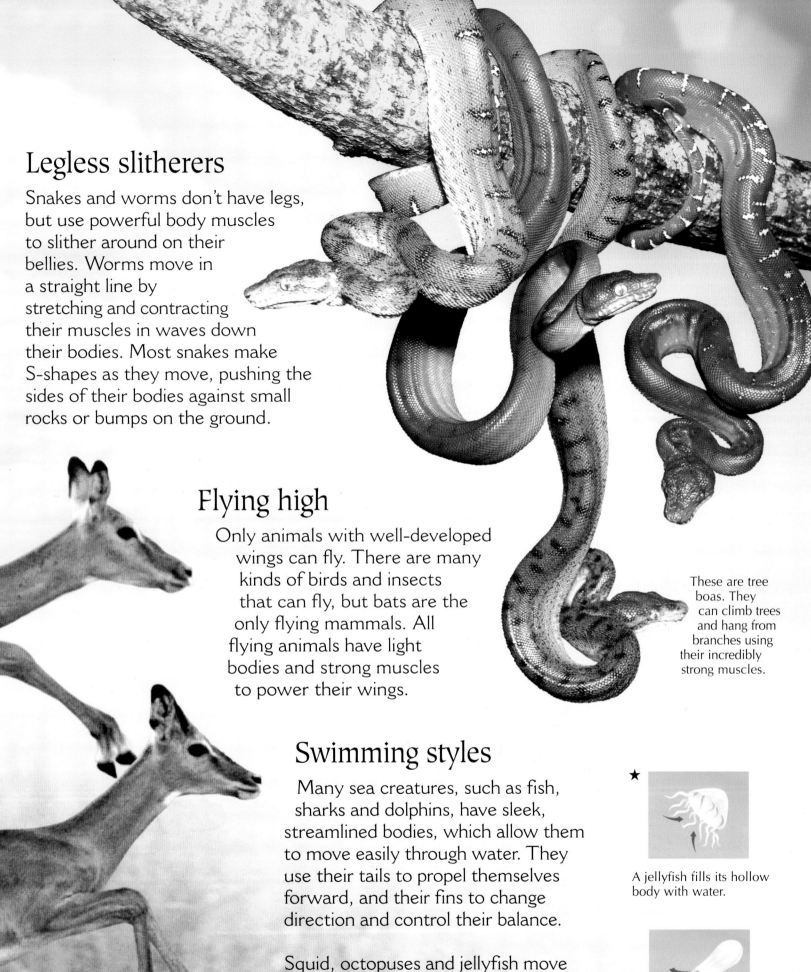

Legless slitherers

Snakes and worms don't have legs, but use powerful body muscles to slither around on their bellies. Worms move in a straight line by stretching and contracting their muscles in waves down their bodies. Most snakes make S-shapes as they move, pushing the sides of their bodies against small rocks or bumps on the ground.

Flying high

Only animals with well-developed wings can fly. There are many kinds of birds and insects that can fly, but bats are the only flying mammals. All flying animals have light bodies and strong muscles to power their wings.

These are tree boas. They can climb trees and hang from branches using their incredibly strong muscles.

Swimming styles

Many sea creatures, such as fish, sharks and dolphins, have sleek, streamlined bodies, which allow them to move easily through water. They use their tails to propel themselves forward, and their fins to change direction and control their balance.

Squid, octopuses and jellyfish move using jet propulsion. They take water into their bodies and then force it out. The action of forcing out the water pushes them in the opposite direction.

A jellyfish fills its hollow body with water.

As the jellyfish pushes the water out, it moves up.

Meal time

All animals need to eat to live. Many animals have teeth for tearing, chewing or grinding up their food. Toothless animals often have beaks for snapping up food, or long, flexible tongues.

Hunting for food

Predators are animals that hunt other animals. They have many different ways of catching their prey (the animals they eat). Some predators use speed and keen eyesight. Others rely on stealth and surprise attacks. All meat-eating animals are known as carnivores.

★

Great white sharks surprise their prey by swimming up to them from below.

Plant munchers

Plant-eaters are known as herbivores. Plants provide less energy than meat, and are also a lot harder to digest. Many herbivores have flat back teeth, which allow them to grind down their food into a pulp, so they can digest it.

This strange-looking monkey is a mandrill. Mandrills snatch leaves from trees and store them in pouches inside their cheeks, until they find a safe spot to eat them.

Internet link

For a link to a website where you can hunt with a lion and see how an animal's physical features help it survive, go to **www.usborne-quicklinks.com**

Bird beaks

Birds use their beaks to catch and carry their food. The size and shape of their beaks are often suited to the food they eat. Birds of prey, such as eagles and owls, have sharp, hooked beaks for tearing meat, while kingfishers' beaks have saw-toothed edges for holding on to slippery fish.

Kingfishers dive into rivers to catch fish. This kingfisher is returning from a successful dive. It will eat its fish once it has found somewhere to perch.

Tongue tactics

Some animals use their tongues to catch food. Snails can scrape food into their mouths just by licking it with their rough tongues. Chameleons catch live prey using their long, sticky tongues. They then snap back their tongues and swallow their victims.

It takes just a fraction of a second for a chameleon to shoot out its tongue and catch an insect. This amazing photograph has caught one in the act.

★ Grasshoppers have jaws like pliers to nip tiny pieces off plants.

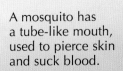

★ A mosquito has a tube-like mouth, used to pierce skin and suck blood.

Bug food

Over half of bugs are plant-eaters, but the rest hunt small animals, often other bugs, for food. There are even bugs that eat dead animals and animal droppings. All bugs have mouths designed to cope with their different diets.

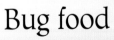

Seeing and hearing

Animals see and hear in many different ways. A seahorse can move its eyes independently of each other, crickets hear through their knees and bats and dolphins can "see" using sound.

Like all dragonflies, this one has compound eyes, which wrap around the sides of its head.

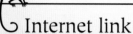

Internet link

For a link to a website where you can see if you can identify some night animals by the sounds they make, go to
www.usborne-quicklinks.com

Bug-eyed

Most bugs have big eyes called compound eyes, which are made up of hundreds of tiny lenses. Each lens sees an individual image. The bug's brain puts together images from all the lenses to make a complete picture. Some bugs have extra eyes called simple eyes, which can sense light and dark.

This mosaic-like image shows how a bug would see a flower through its compound eyes.

Night sight

Night animals, also known as nocturnal animals, often have enormous eyes for the size of their bodies. This is so that the slit in the middle of the eye, called the pupil, can open very wide, to let in as much light as possible. This helps nocturnal animals to see in the dark.

These are slender lorises. Both the mother's and baby's pupils have shrunk to small circles, so they aren't dazzled by the bright light of the camera.

Looking out

Animals have eyes in different positions on their heads. Herbivores usually have eyes on the sides of their heads, so they can look out for predators as they feed. Many predators, such as owls, foxes and tigers, have eyes that face forward. As a result, they can focus on a wide area with both eyes at the same time, giving them clearer vision. This is called binocular vision, and it is how people see.

The purple triangle shows an owl's area of binocular vision. The lighter area shows how far around an owl can see without moving its head.

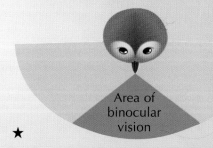

Area of binocular vision

★

This owl has used its sharp eyesight to spot a mouse in the dark. Its claws are opened wide, ready to grab it.

Good vibrations

All animals hear by detecting air movements called sound waves. Most animals have openings known as outer ears that channel sound waves into the body. Mammals have ears on their heads, while most insects have ears on their bodies or legs. Snakes don't have ears and are deaf, but they can detect vibrations in the ground made by other animals.

Mice have big ears to help them hear well. But owls have silent wingbeats, so this mouse hasn't heard the owl approaching.

★

A bat sends out high-pitched sounds.

The echo tells the bat that prey is nearby.

Seeing sound

Bats and dolphins use sound to find their way around and hunt for food. They send out high-pitched sounds, which bounce off nearby objects and return to the animal as an echo. The animal uses the echo to find out exactly where an object is.

Smell, taste and touch

Different animals smell, taste and touch with different parts of their bodies. There are fish that can detect smells all over their bodies, butterflies that taste with their feet and mammals that can detect the faintest touch using hairs on their faces.

Tactile tentacles

Many sea creatures and soft-bodied animals, such as snails and slugs, have long, flexible body parts called tentacles, which they use to catch food and feel their way around. Sea anemones have stinging tentacles. They use them to paralyze prey, which makes the prey easier to catch.

★
A sea anenome uses its tentacles to sting fish.

It then grabs the fish and pulls it into its mouth.

This is a large rodent called a paca. You can see how it has whiskers both around its nose and behind its eyes. Pacas are nocturnal, so they need their whiskers to navigate their way in the dark.

Whiskery touch

Long, stiff hairs called whiskers help mammals to detect faint movements in the air and to feel their way in the dark, or through dense vegetation. They also use their whiskers to test the width of narrow spaces. If a mammal can get its whiskers through a gap, it knows the rest of its body will probably fit through as well.

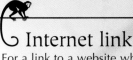
Internet link

For a link to a website where you can read about some animals' super senses, go to **www.usborne-quicklinks.com**

Flicking tongues

Most animals detect smells using their nostrils. But some animals, including snakes, also have special smell detectors, called Jacobson's organs, on the roofs of their mouths.

Snakes use their tongues to pick up smells in the air. When a snake pushes its tongue over its Jacobson's organ, it can tell what the smell is. When hunting, snakes use their forked tongues to tell if prey is to the left or to the right, depending which side of its tongue picks up a stronger scent.

This green rat snake is flicking out its tongue to taste the air. It can use its tongue to identify animals nearby, even if it can't see them.

This cutaway diagram of a snake's head shows the Jacobson's organ on the roof of its mouth.

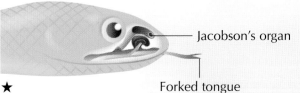

Jacobson's organ

Forked tongue

★

Antennae action

Insects and other arthropods, such as crabs and shrimps, have jointed, flexible feelers, or antennae, on their heads. These are highly sensitive to touch, and are also covered in tiny hairs that pick up smells in the air. Some animals can also taste with their antennae.

This is a weevil, a kind of beetle. The two bent, stick-like things coming off its long snout are its antennae.

Tasty feet

The senses of smell and taste usually work together and animals mostly detect taste in their mouths. Insects, though, can detect taste in other places, even on the ends of their legs. This means they can taste their food just by walking on it.

Animal talk

Animals talk to each other using a mixture of smells, sounds and signs. Even the shades and patterns on an animal's body can send out a message. Most messages are to do with finding mates or giving warnings to other animals.

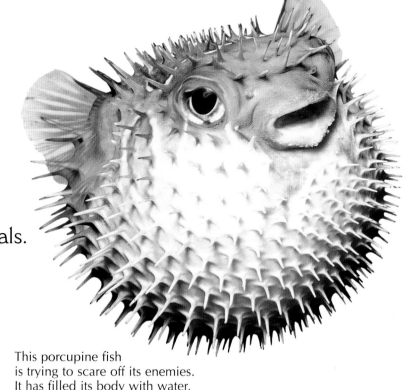

This porcupine fish is trying to scare off its enemies. It has filled its body with water, to appear bigger than it really is.

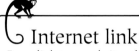

Internet link

For a link to a website where you can see video clips of bees waggle dancing and find out more about the dance, go to **www.usborne-quicklinks.com**

Bright warnings

No animal wants to be eaten. Poisonous and foul-tasting animals often have bright markings, to let predators know they would be harmful to eat. Some can even change their appearance. When threatened, blue-ringed octopuses switch from dull to bright yellow, to warn predators away. Predators usually do try to avoid them, as each one has enough poison to kill 25 men.

Body language

Animals that live in groups often have complex systems of signs to communicate with each other. Honeybees, for example, perform a dance known as a waggle dance in the shape of the figure 8, to let other bees know where to find food. In the waggle dance, the more frequent the waggles, the nearer the source of the food.

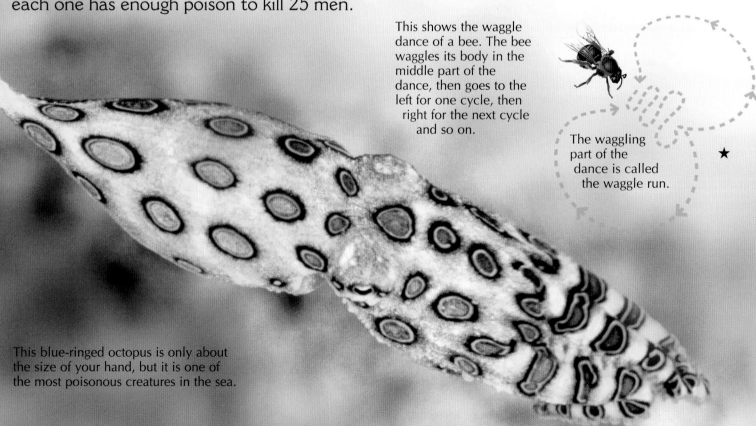

This shows the waggle dance of a bee. The bee waggles its body in the middle part of the dance, then goes to the left for one cycle, then right for the next cycle and so on.

The waggling part of the dance is called the waggle run.

This blue-ringed octopus is only about the size of your hand, but it is one of the most poisonous creatures in the sea.

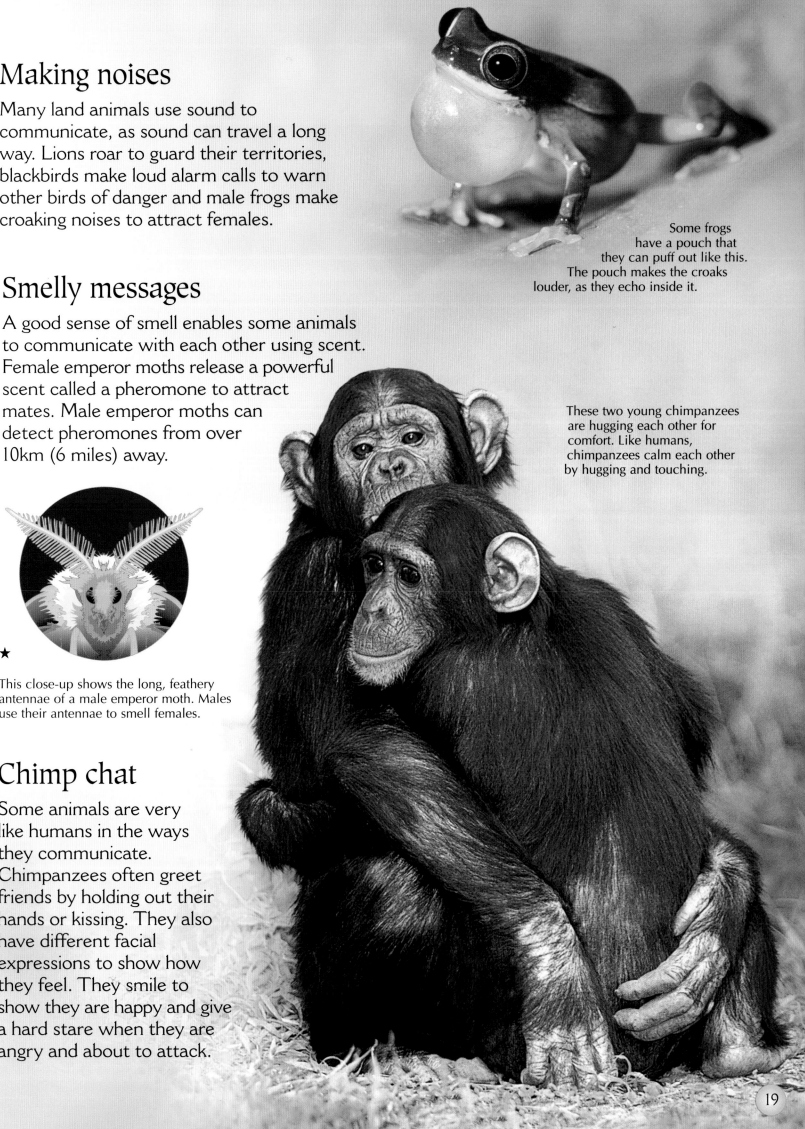

Making noises

Many land animals use sound to communicate, as sound can travel a long way. Lions roar to guard their territories, blackbirds make loud alarm calls to warn other birds of danger and male frogs make croaking noises to attract females.

Some frogs have a pouch that they can puff out like this. The pouch makes the croaks louder, as they echo inside it.

Smelly messages

A good sense of smell enables some animals to communicate with each other using scent. Female emperor moths release a powerful scent called a pheromone to attract mates. Male emperor moths can detect pheromones from over 10km (6 miles) away.

These two young chimpanzees are hugging each other for comfort. Like humans, chimpanzees calm each other by hugging and touching.

★

This close-up shows the long, feathery antennae of a male emperor moth. Males use their antennae to smell females.

Chimp chat

Some animals are very like humans in the ways they communicate. Chimpanzees often greet friends by holding out their hands or kissing. They also have different facial expressions to show how they feel. They smile to show they are happy and give a hard stare when they are angry and about to attack.

Getting together

The majority of animals need to find partners in order to mate and have young. This is called breeding. Good breeding places and suitable partners can be hard to find, especially when there is lots of competition around. Animals use a whole range of tricks and strategies to beat their rivals.

Internet link
For a link to a website where you can listen to birds singing to attract mates, go to www.usborne-quicklinks.com

Fighting it out

Fights can break out between rival males trying to mate with the same female. Goats battle with their horns, while male deer clash antlers. Some fights, however, are just for display. Male rattlesnakes rear up and wrap themselves around one another. Each snake tries to wrestle the other to the ground, but they never actually harm each other.

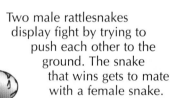

Two male rattlesnakes display fight by trying to push each other to the ground. The snake that wins gets to mate with a female snake.

Showing off

In the bird world, it is also usually the males that have to impress the females. Breeding generally takes place in spring, when males look their finest. They perform courtship displays to attract female attention. These often involve singing and dancing, or spreading out their feathers to show off their plumage.

By lifting his bright blue feet up and down, this male blue-footed booby is hoping to attract the attention of a female.

This weaver bird is putting the finishing touches to his nest. Once it is finished, he will flap his wings to attract a female.

Hard to please

There are birds that have to go to a lot of effort to attract mates. Male weaver birds construct intricate nests out of strips of grass, which they weave together with their beaks and feet. A female weaver bird then inspects the nest to see if it's good enough. If not, the male destroys his nest and starts all over again.

The weaver bird starts by weaving a simple loop of grass onto a branch.

Gradually, he weaves in more grass to make the nest bigger.

He leaves an entrance hole at the bottom to get in and out.

Pairing and sharing

Most animals don't stay together after mating. A male red deer mates with many females and doesn't stay around to look after his young. But there are a few animals that form lifelong pairs. Jackals, for example, stay together for life, and both parents look after their pups, guarding them closely and teaching them to hunt.

A pair of black-backed jackals groom each other as a sign of affection.

Growing up

Baby animals can look like tiny versions of their parents. However others go through amazing changes as they grow up. Some baby animals depend completely on their parents to feed and protect them, but most are born ready to fend for themselves.

Internet link

For a link to a website where you can watch video clips of baby animals, go to **www.usborne-quicklinks.com**

Body changes

Amphibians, such as frogs and newts, lay eggs, known as spawn. The spawn is covered by a soft, jelly-like substance that protects and nourishes it. At first, baby amphibians look nothing like their parents, but grow to look more like them, developing first legs, then lungs, so they can live both in and out of water.

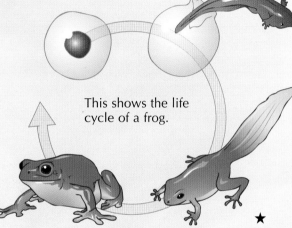

At first, a frog's egg looks like a tiny black dot.

The egg hatches into a tadpole.

This shows the life cycle of a frog.

Eventually, its tail disappears and it becomes a frog.

The tadpole grows four legs.

Hatching eggs

Almost all birds sit on their eggs for two weeks or more, to protect them and keep them warm. When a baby bird is ready to hatch, it chips its way out of the egg, using a lump on its beak called an egg tooth. Most baby birds need a lot of care from their parents, as they are born blind and without any feathers.

A baby emperor penguin nestles close to its parents for warmth. It is still covered in fluffy down, and has yet to grow its thick covering of adult feathers.

Growing wings

Bugs usually lay eggs and leave them to hatch alone. Butterflies, for example, lay their eggs on leaves and then fly away. The eggs hatch into tiny caterpillars, which feed on the plants around them. When a caterpillar is fully grown, it attaches itself to a plant and grows a hard outer skin, called a pupa. Inside, the adult butterfly develops and grows wings, then breaks free.

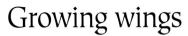

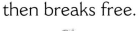

This amazing series of photographs shows a painted lady butterfly hatching out of its pupa and flying away.

Snake nests

Most reptiles lay their eggs in hidden places and never return. But a few snakes, such as king cobras, build nests and guard their eggs until they hatch.

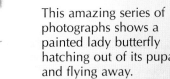

A king cobra makes a nest out of leaves, lays her eggs on top of the pile, then wraps her body around them.

Baby mammals

At first, all baby mammals rely on their mothers for food, and stay with them until they can fend for themselves. There are usually close links between a mother and her young, so young mammals can learn by copying their mothers.

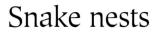

Even lions are helpless when young. This lioness is carrying her cub from one spot to another, to put any predators off the scent.

Journeys and rest

All animals face the same challenge in life: to grow up and have babies before they die. But survival can be hard, and every season brings new difficulties. Animals cope in different ways. Some go on long journeys. Others hide away from harsh weather until it improves.

Mapping the way

Animals often travel extremely long distances to breed or find food. This is called migrating. Many animals migrate twice every year, to their breeding or feeding grounds and back. No one is certain how migrating animals find their way. They may use landmarks such as mountains and rivers, or they may use the position of the sun and stars to help them.

Flying formations

Migrating in large groups can provide protection from predators. For birds, migrating in groups can also make their journey easier. Geese fly in V-shaped formations. As each goose flaps its wings, a spiralling updraft of air spreads out from the tips of the wings. This updraft provides a boost for the goose above it, helping it to save energy as it flies.

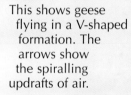

This shows geese flying in a V-shaped formation. The arrows show the spiralling updrafts of air.

★

Turtle travel

Some animals are faced with a momentous journey from the moment they are born. Female loggerhead turtles lay their eggs on beaches in eastern Florida, in the USA. When the eggs hatch two months later, the tiny hatchlings head for the sea. It is the beginning of a 13,000km (8,000 mile) trip, which takes them to their feeding grounds and then back to the beach where they were born.

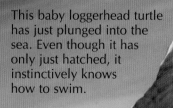

This baby loggerhead turtle has just plunged into the sea. Even though it has only just hatched, it instinctively knows how to swim.

★

Immediately after hatching, baby turtles make their way to the sea.

Years later, female turtles return to the same beach to lay their eggs.

These grizzly bears are fishing for migrating salmon, catching them in their jaws as they leap upstream.

Leaping salmon

Salmon undergo one of the most arduous of all migrations. They travel upstream from the sea to the rivers where they hatched, battling against the current and even leaping up waterfalls to get there. When they arrive, the females lay eggs, or spawn, on the riverbed, in hollows dug out with their tails. Most females die from exhaustion after spawning. Less than 1% return to the sea and survive to spawn a second time.

Sleepy snakes

During cold winter months, many animals, including toads, bears and snakes, hide away in a safe place to sleep. Sleeping through winter is called hibernation. Animals don't need to eat during this time, as their body fat gives them enough energy to stay alive until spring.

Internet link

For a link to a website where you can play a bird migration game, go to **www.usborne-quicklinks.com**

These red-sided garter snakes are emerging from their winter burrow. One has flicked out its tongue for its first taste of spring.

Living together

No animal lives completely alone. Some live in large groups where they all share the work. Others keep mostly to themselves, only getting together to breed. But all animals must interact with many other species in their daily lives.

Food chains

Animals and plants live together in communities known as ecosystems. In an ecosystem, animals are linked together by what they eat – one species eats another, and is in turn eaten by another. This is called a food chain. Decomposers are at the bottom of the chain. They break down dead plants and animals and return minerals to the soil.

Carnivores, the meat-eaters, are at the top of a food chain.

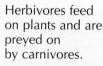

Herbivores feed on plants and are preyed on by carnivores.

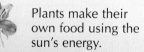

Plants make their own food using the sun's energy.

Decomposers, such as fungi and bacteria, feed on dead plants and animals.

★

Helping out

Sometimes, two different kinds of animal help each other to survive. Clown fish have a coating of slime on their skin that allows them to live among poisonous sea anemones without being stung. This protects them from predators. The clown fish attract prey for the sea anemone and clean its tentacles.

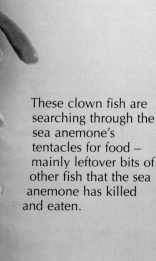

These clown fish are searching through the sea anemone's tentacles for food – mainly leftover bits of other fish that the sea anemone has killed and eaten.

Bee jobs

Animals that live together in highly structured groups are known as social animals. Each member of a group has its own job to do. In a hive of honeybees, for example, the queen lays the eggs, the drones (males) mate with the queen and the workers (females) find food.

These worker honeybees are depositing nectar from flowers, as a food store for winter.

Internet link

For a link to a website where you can watch a short movie about food chains and do a quiz, go to **www.usborne-quicklinks.com**

Pest control

Partnerships are often formed between small and large animals. Oxpeckers, for example, are birds that live on large mammals and comb through their hair, picking out blood-sucking insects, such as ticks and fleas. This helps keep the mammal healthy and provides oxpeckers with a good meal.

This sable antelope is letting an oxpecker search inside its ear for ticks. You can just see another oxpecker, below the antelope's chin.

A place in the crowd

Animals that live in large groups must be able to find their partners among the crowd. To us, 5,000 gannets packed together on a cliff top may seem identical, but each gannet can tell its partner's call from all the others, and can remember the exact location of its nest.

When gannets find their partners they touch beaks, like this, to show that they recognize each other.

Hide and seek

Many animals have patterns on their bodies that enable them to blend in with their surroundings, or to trick predators into thinking they are another kind of animal. This is known as camouflage. Camouflage helps animals to find food and avoid attack.

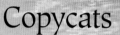

Masters of change

Chameleons are usually green and speckled, so they blend in perfectly against their leafy environment. But they alter the patterns on their skin if there's a change in the temperature, or if they want to communicate with other animals.

A chameleon gives itself bright stripes to warn an enemy that it's angry.

It turns brown when it's cold. Being darker allows it to absorb more heat from the sun.

★

Seasonal coats

Some mammals can change their coats to match the seasons. In winter, snowshoe hares, for example, go from brown to white, so they blend in with the snow.

This snowshoe hare is halfway through its coat change. The white winter fur always appears first on its ears and feet.

Copycats

Instead of blending in with their environment, some harmless animals look like poisonous animals, so they won't be eaten. This is known as mimicry. Monarch butterflies, for example, are poisonous for other animals to eat. This is because they grow up feeding on milkweed, which makes most animals sick. Harmless viceroy butterflies look almost exactly like them, so predators avoid them too.

★

Can you spot the difference between a viceroy and a monarch butterfly? The viceroy butterfly has an extra black stripe on its wings.

When zebras stand together like this, their stripes can confuse a predator. The stripes of the whole herd merge, making it hard for a predator to pick out a single animal to chase.

Breaking up

The pattern on an animal's coat can help to break up its outline, making it harder to spot. Most animals see in black and white, so although an animal's patterns may make it easier for us to see, they help to hide it from other predators. To a lion, for example, a zebra's black and white striped coat makes it blend in with long grasses.

Flower power

Some animals are so well camouflaged it's almost impossible to see them. Flower mantises, for example, are predatory insects that can match their surroundings perfectly. They look so like flowers that insects land on them to get nectar. The mantis then snaps out its claws and eats the insects.

⌒ Internet link
For a link to a website where you can play a game to find out about different kinds of camouflage, go to **www.usborne-quicklinks.com**

This is a flower mantis. Its pink body and petal-shaped legs make it look exactly like a pink orchid flower. You can see the jagged edges on its front claws, which help it to grip its prey.

29

These Honduran white bats have made this leaf into a shelter. Roosting under a leaf helps to keep them safe and dry.

Animal homes

An animal's immediate surroundings are called its habitat. Within a habitat, there are many places where an animal can make its home. Some animals build permanent homes, while others only find places to shelter when they have young.

This tree frog is laying its eggs inside a water-filled leafcup. It chooses the leafcup carefully, making sure there is enough water in it for when the eggs hatch into tadpoles.

Building work

Animals can be amazingly skilled at building homes, making elaborate structures from all kinds of materials. Termites build huge mounds, 6m (20ft) high, out of soil, saliva and droppings, while some bats can make tents out of leaves. These leaf-tents can last for up to year.

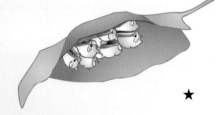

★

A tent-making bat bites holes along the spine of a leaf.

The holes cause the two sides of the leaf to droop down, forming a tent where the bats can roost.

Ready-made shelters

Some animals don't build homes at all, but rely on their surroundings for safety and shelter. Squirrels sleep in holes in trees, while koalas sleep wedged in the crooks of trees, away from most predators. Tree frogs find ready-made homes high up in the rainforest, in leafcups that fill up with rainwater.

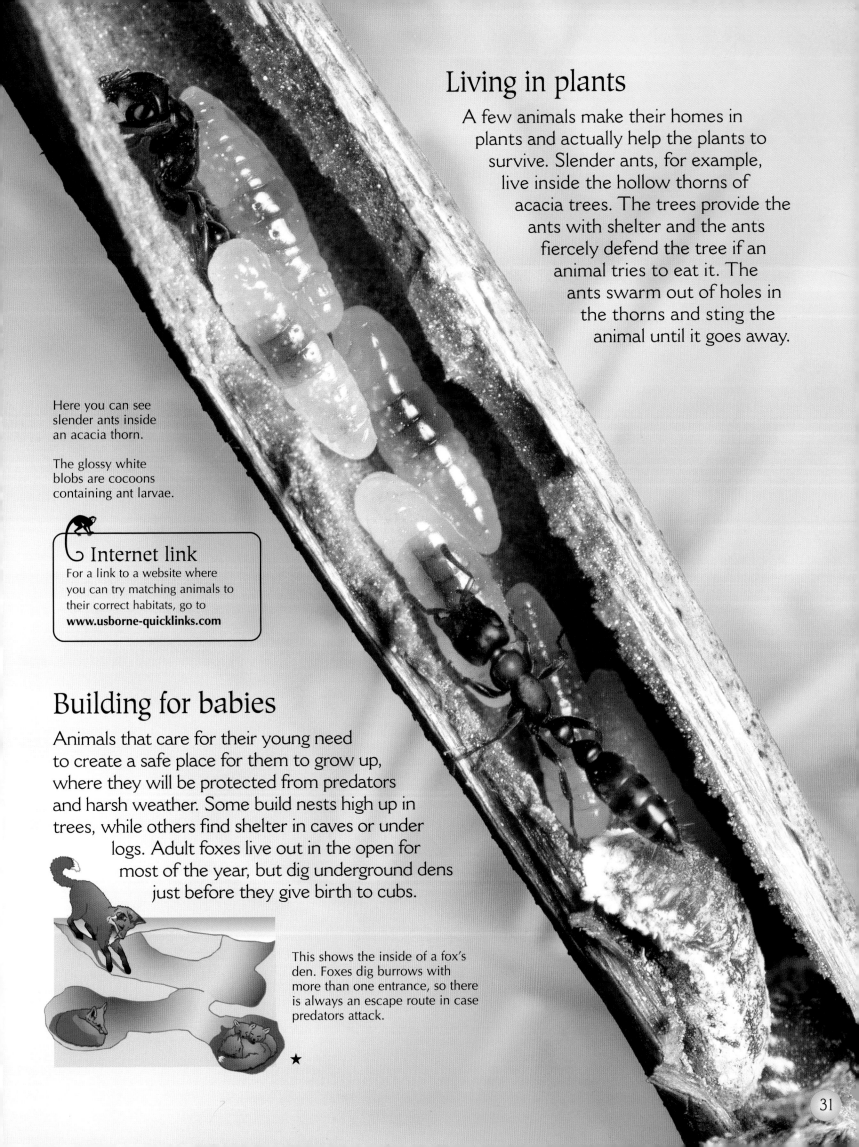

Living in plants

A few animals make their homes in plants and actually help the plants to survive. Slender ants, for example, live inside the hollow thorns of acacia trees. The trees provide the ants with shelter and the ants fiercely defend the tree if an animal tries to eat it. The ants swarm out of holes in the thorns and sting the animal until it goes away.

Here you can see slender ants inside an acacia thorn.

The glossy white blobs are cocoons containing ant larvae.

Internet link

For a link to a website where you can try matching animals to their correct habitats, go to **www.usborne-quicklinks.com**

Building for babies

Animals that care for their young need to create a safe place for them to grow up, where they will be protected from predators and harsh weather. Some build nests high up in trees, while others find shelter in caves or under logs. Adult foxes live out in the open for most of the year, but dig underground dens just before they give birth to cubs.

This shows the inside of a fox's den. Foxes dig burrows with more than one entrance, so there is always an escape route in case predators attack.

★

Conservation

Many animal species are in danger of dying out completely. This is known as becoming extinct. Some animals are hunted for fur or meat, but the biggest threat faced by most animals is the loss of their habitat. Nature conservation aims to protect plants and animals, and preserve their habitats.

Fast disappearing

Since life on Earth began, species have died out as a result of natural changes in the world. But, for thousands of years, until the beginning of the twentieth century, less than one species in a million became extinct each year. Since then, human activity has led to a huge increase in that number, with between 1,000 and 10,000 species in a million now becoming extinct each year.

Unknown animals

Scientists estimate there are around 10 million animal species, but only 1.2 million of those have been named and described by scientists. This means that each year there are species becoming extinct that have never even been discovered.

This is a golden lion tamarin. These monkeys are extremely rare, as their rainforest homes have been chopped down. In the 1970s, there were only 200 left in the wild. Through conservation efforts there are now around 1,000.

Tracking animals

By studying animals, scientists can learn how best to try to save them. Animals are often tagged so scientists can track their movements, although advances in technology mean that larger animals can now be fitted with radio transmitters. These give out electronic signals, so scientists can follow an animal's movements even more accurately.

Birds are tagged with a small ring around the leg.

Mammals are fitted with radio collars around the neck.

This scientist is inserting a transmitter into a tiger shark. The shark has to be tranquilized first, so it doesn't attack him.

Captive breeding

Sometimes, species become so rare that the only way to stop them from dying out is to breed them in captivity, such as in nature reserves or zoos. This has helped boost the numbers of many rare animal species, including golden lion tamarins, wattled cranes, parrots and falcons, as well as the last breed of wild horse. Captive breeding also helps to make people more aware and concerned about endangered animals.

Returning to the wild

It is very difficult to return captive animals to their natural habitats in the wild, as they may lack the skills they need to survive. Conservationists go to great lengths to train some animals to return to the wild. Animals must learn to find their own food, to communicate with other members of their species and not to rely on humans.

This man has made his arm into a puppet of a wattled crane, so that the crane chick thinks the puppet is its mother. This will help the crane to interact with other cranes in the wild.

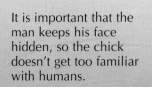

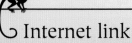

Internet link

For a link to a website where you can find what makes some animals become extinct, go to
www.usborne-quicklinks.com

It is important that the man keeps his face hidden, so the chick doesn't get too familiar with humans.

South and Central America

The Amazon rainforest, at the heart of South America, is home to more animals than anywhere else on Earth. Elsewhere on the continent there are mammals that are covered in scales, camels with the finest wool in the world and a spectacular variety of birds.

Blue morpho butterflies, from the Amazon, have amazing iridescent blue wings.

Toucans

The rainforest canopy (pages 38–39)

GUATEMALA
EL SALVADOR
HONDURAS
NICARAGUA
BELIZE
COSTA RICA
PANAMA

Resplendent quetzal

ECUADOR

VENEZUELA

COLOMBIA

Cock-of-the-rock

GUYANA
SURINAM
FRENCH GUIANA (France)

Amazon kingfisher

Flying fish

Three-toed sloth

Tree anteater

AMAZON

Scarlet macaw

PERU

Andes Mountains (pages 36–37)

BOLIVIA

Jaguar

The Amazon (pages 40–41)

Caiman

Capybara

BRAZIL

Giant anteater

Grassland life (pages 42–43)

Rhea

Coral snake

Common marmoset

Frigate bird

GALAPAGOS ISLANDS

Blue-footed booby

Map key

Forests
Mountains
Deserts
Other (grassland, farmland & cities)

This map shows just some of the animals that live in South America.

A black-handed spider monkey can swing from a branch by its tail, leaving its hands free for feeding.

Handy tails

Many South American animals, including tree anteaters and spider monkeys, have prehensile tails. This means they can use their tails like a fifth limb, to grip onto branches. Some monkeys can even use their tails to pick up objects.

Bird life

Over a third of the world's bird species breed in South America, and many others migrate there in winter. Some of the most spectacular species include hyacinth macaws, the largest kind of parrot, resplendent quetzals, whose tail feathers were once worn by Mayan kings, and Andean condors, which have wings measuring 3m (10ft) from tip to tip.

Here you can see four parrot species from Central and South America. There are over 150 different species in total.

Blue and yellow macaw

Scarlet macaw

Hyacinth macaw

Golden conure

PARAGUAY

URUGUAY

ARGENTINA

CHILE

Thirteen-banded armadillo

Mara

Chinchilla

Mountain viscacha

Guanacos

Andean condor

Internet link

For links to websites where you can listen to animals in the Amazon rainforest and find out more about South American animals, go to **www.usborne-quicklinks.com**

Galapagos islands

The Galapagos are a group of islands around 1,000km (620 miles) off South America's west coast. As a result of being so remote, there are animal species on the islands found nowhere else in the world. These include giant tortoises, Darwin's finches, lava lizards and marine iguanas – the only species of sea lizard.

All marine iguanas have these long, sharp claws so they can grip onto rocks and not be washed away.

These sally lightfoot crabs are scuttling over the Galapagos' black rocks. They are climbing crabs, using the long spines on the ends of their legs to cling to the wave-battered rocks.

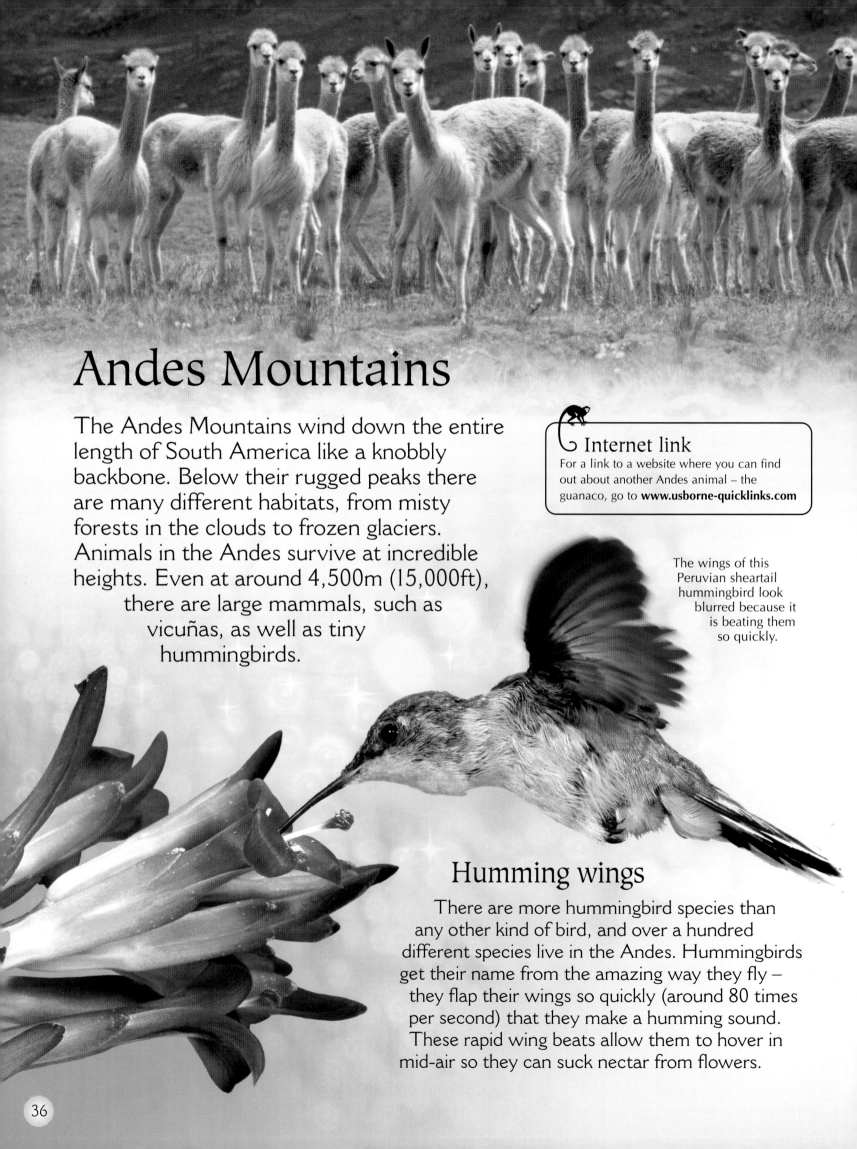

Andes Mountains

The Andes Mountains wind down the entire length of South America like a knobbly backbone. Below their rugged peaks there are many different habitats, from misty forests in the clouds to frozen glaciers. Animals in the Andes survive at incredible heights. Even at around 4,500m (15,000ft), there are large mammals, such as vicuñas, as well as tiny hummingbirds.

Internet link
For a link to a website where you can find out about another Andes animal – the guanaco, go to **www.usborne-quicklinks.com**

The wings of this Peruvian sheartail hummingbird look blurred because it is beating them so quickly.

Humming wings

There are more hummingbird species than any other kind of bird, and over a hundred different species live in the Andes. Hummingbirds get their name from the amazing way they fly – they flap their wings so quickly (around 80 times per second) that they make a humming sound. These rapid wing beats allow them to hover in mid-air so they can suck nectar from flowers.

This herd of vicuñas is on a grassy plain in the Andes. Although their coats may look thin, they are made up of insulating hairs that are softer and warmer than any other animal hair in the world.

Small camels

Vicuñas are the smallest kind of camel. They live high up in the Andes in groups led by a single male. They are very vocal animals, warning each other of danger with high-pitched whinnies and greeting each other with soft humming sounds. Males also make throaty noises known as "orgling" to attract mates.

Bear nests

Spectacled bears are the only bears in South America. They live in the misty forests on the lower slopes of the Andes. Like many bears, they are very good climbers. They often build nests in trees, which they use for sleeping and as a base to reach for food.

A spectacled bear makes its nest out of layers of branches and twigs. The nest allows the bear to get at leaves it otherwise wouldn't be able to reach.

You can see the bold patterns on this spectacled bear's face. This is how the bear gets its name, as the patterns make some bears look like they're wearing glasses.

The rainforest canopy

In rainforests, the tree tops form a roof known as the canopy. Some animals make a daily journey from the forest floor to the canopy, to get their share of its rich supply of food. Others spend all their lives in the canopy and need never come down.

Internet link

For a link to a website where you can read amazing facts about leafcutter ants and see them in action, go to www.usborne-quicklinks.com

Big beak

The huge, bright beak of the toco toucan is a useful tool in the canopy, helping it to reach out and pluck fruit from branches that are too thin to stand on. Toucans live in small, noisy flocks and nest together in hollow trees.

The size of this toco toucan's beak can easily unbalance it, making it a poor flier. Instead of flying, toucans spend most of their time hopping between branches.

Fungus food

Leafcutter ants live in enormous groups, called colonies, on the forest floor. Some members of the colony have to travel huge distances each day to collect leaves from high up in the canopy. They use the leaves to grow a special kind of fungus to feed the entire colony.

Leafcutter ants haul leaves back to their nest by balancing them between their jaws and antennae.

The kinkajou uses its long, stretchy tongue to sip nectar from flowers.

Night climbers

Kinkajous act like monkeys, but they are more closely related to raccoons. They move quickly through the canopy, leaping through the air, then gripping onto branches with their long, prehensile tails. Kinkajous come out to feed at night. They eat fruit, tree sap and nectar, which they lap up with their 15cm (6in) long tongues.

Unusually, this photograph shows a sloth in mid-movement. Sloths stay still for up to 20 hours a day.

Slow progress

Three-toed sloths spend nearly all their lives upside down, hanging from branches by their powerful, hook-like claws. They move so slowly that algae grows on their fur, giving them a greenish tinge. This helps to camouflage them among the leaves. Sloths also lick the algae, as it provides them with nutrients.

Poisonous frogs

Poison-dart frogs are tiny but deadly. Their bright markings warn predators that their skin is poisonous to touch. They live on the rainforest floor, but lay their eggs in pools of water in leaves in the canopy. They get to the canopy by jumping from branch to branch and gripping with suction cups on their toes.

These are strawberry poison-dart frogs. They only grow to the size of a bumblebee.

The Amazon

Deep in the Amazon rainforest, the mighty
Amazon River splits up into over a thousand
smaller rivers and streams. This area is home
to countless species of animals. Some spend
their time in the water, while others look
for food on the swampy forest floor.
The air is constantly filled with the
loud screeching of macaws and
the chirps and cries of monkeys.

Canopy chorus

Howler monkeys are the loudest
land animals. They live in groups
high in the canopy and only ever
come down to the forest floor
to drink. Every day, at dawn,
each group breaks into a
deafening howling chorus to
mark its territory. Their calls can
be heard up to 5km (3 miles) away.

This is a red howler monkey. Red howler
monkeys are among the largest monkeys in South
America, growing up to 1.2m (4ft) long.

Internet link
For a link to a website where
you can go on a virtual tour of
the Amazon rainforest, go to
www.usborne-quicklinks.com

Coiled killers

Anacondas are enormous snakes. They
ambush prey by lying in wait, either in
shallow water or coiled up on overhanging
branches. They kill by winding around their
victims, and then using powerful muscles to
squeeze them until they can no longer
breathe. After a good meal, an anaconda
can go for over a year without eating.

An anaconda first wraps
itself in coils around its
prey to suffocate it.

It then stretches its jaws
to swallow its prey, usually headfirst. This takes it several hours.

Nut cracker

Scarlet macaws are large rainforest parrots with incredibly bright feathers. They feed on fruit and nuts, using their feet like hands to hold their food. Their hooked beaks are strong enough to crack the shell of the toughest nut of all, the Brazil nut, which no other bird can eat.

Climbing chicks

Unlike other birds, hoatzin chicks have claws on their wings. The claws help them to climb trees. Some scientists think hoatzins may be a link between modern birds and prehistoric birds such as archaeopteryx, which also had wing claws. Hoatzins lose their claws before they reach adulthood, as they fuse together with the wing bone.

Claw

Claw

★

A sharp claw on the front of each wing gives young hoatzins a firm grip.

A scarlet macaw dangles like an acrobat while searching for fruit.

A capybara wades through a river. The bird on its head is hitching a lift in order to look out for insects to eat.

Enormous rodents

Capybaras are the world's largest rodents, growing to around the size of a sheep. They graze in family groups around the water's edge, feeding on grasses and water plants. As soon as a capybara senses danger, it barks to alert the rest of the group and they all dive into the water, crowding together for safety.

This campo flicker is perched by the entrance to its nest, which is inside a termite mound.

Grassland life

A huge range of insects live on the South American grasslands, including flies, beetles and butterflies. But the most dominant species are termites and ants. These provide food for large animals, such as armadillos and anteaters, as well as hundreds of birds.

Mounds and ovens

There are very few trees on the grasslands, making it hard for birds to find places to nest. Campo flickers, a type of woodpecker, nest in abandoned termite mounds. Ovenbirds build their own nests, either on the ground or on top of fence posts. The nests are shaped like old-fashioned ovens, with a domed top and a narrow entrance tunnel.

Male and female ovenbirds work together to build their nest, using pieces of wet clay and grass.

Bony balls

Armadillos are covered with thick shells made up of bony plates called scutes. Unlike other armadillos, three-banded armadillos can protect themselves against predators by rolling up into tight balls, so that just their bony plates are exposed. Only jaguars are strong enough to force open the armadillos and eat them.

A three-banded armadillo's plates cover its entire body, apart from its belly.

When rolled up, it can hide its head, legs and tail within its shell.

Long claws and sticky tongues

Giant anteaters have front claws that are too long to walk on. Instead, they tuck them under their feet and walk on their knuckles. They use their claws to tear holes in ant nests and termite mounds. Anteaters then feed by flicking their long sticky tongues into nests to catch insects.

Internet link

For a link to a website where you can watch fantastic video clips of anteaters, go to **www.usborne-quicklinks.com**

★ A giant anteater only makes a small hole in a nest, like this. It is careful not to destroy the nest, so that it can come back to feed on it another time.

These giant anteaters are rooting around for insects. One of the reasons they look so odd is because of the way they feed – their long, tube-like snouts contain the long, sticky tongues they use for catching insects.

North America

North America stretches from the Arctic to the tropics. Bears and wolves roam the frozen north, while alligators and snakes dwell in the steamy swamps of the south. Humans have destroyed much of the natural environment, but have also created national parks to preserve some of the amazing wildlife that is left.

Great migrations

Many animals migrate thousands of miles across North America each year. Snow geese fly from their Arctic summer breeding grounds to marshlands in the south, while monarch butterflies fly over 3,200km (2,000 miles) from the USA to Mexico, in order to escape harsh winter weather.

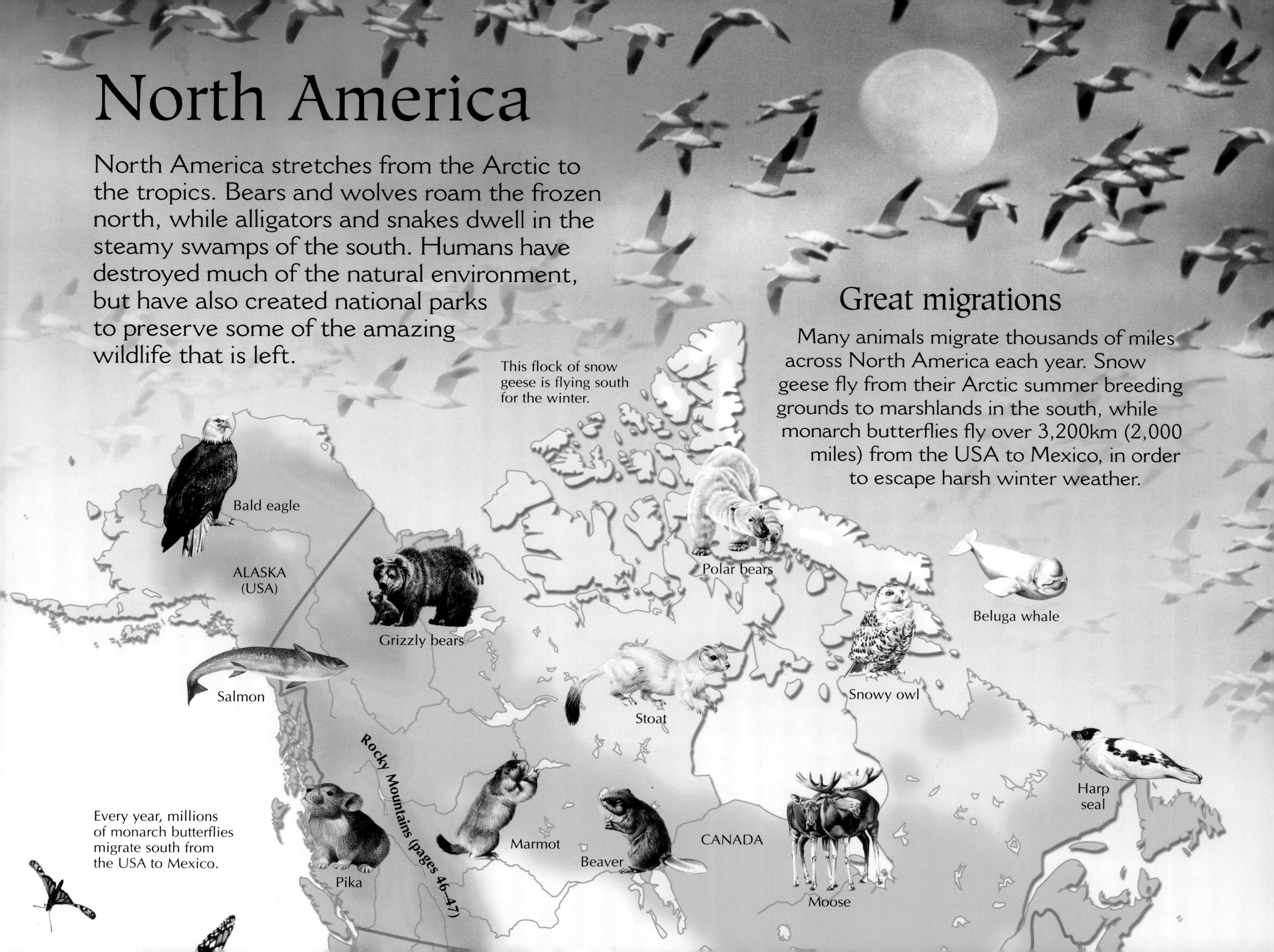

This flock of snow geese is flying south for the winter.

Harp seal

Beluga whale

Snowy owl

Moose

Polar bears

Stoat

CANADA

Beaver

Marmot

Grizzly bears

Rocky Mountains (pages 46–47)

Pika

Bald eagle

ALASKA (USA)

Salmon

Every year, millions of monarch butterflies migrate south from the USA to Mexico.

Map key

- Forests
- Deserts
- Mountains
- Tundra
- Ice & snow
- Other (grassland, farmland & cities)

This map shows just some of the animals that live in North America.

DOMINICAN REPUBLIC

HAITI

JAMAICA

CUBA

Manatee

Florida Everglades (pages 52–53)

Garpike

Cottonmouth

Raccoon

Bison

Coyote

The prairies (pages 48–49)

Prairie dog

Elf owl

Poison-dart frog

MEXICO

Rattlesnake

Vampire bat

Sonoran Desert (pages 50–51)

Roadrunner

Timber wolf

UNITED STATES OF AMERICA

Sea lion

Internet link

For links to websites packed with animal facts and photographs from North America, go to **www.usborne-quicklinks.com**

This shows a beaver home, known as a lodge. Beavers build their lodges out of sticks and mud. The entrance tunnels are underwater.

Raccoon raiders

The spread of towns, cities and farmland across North America has brought many animals close to extinction. Raccoons, however, have adapted amazingly well to the changing environment. They feed on anything from frogs to fruit, and will climb in through windows, lift latches and even raid from cupboards in their search for food.

Raccoons are often nicknamed "masked bandits" because of this mask-like pattern around their eyes, and their habit of stealing food.

Beaver dams

Some animals have a much greater impact on the environment than others, and beavers have one of the greatest of all. They have strong teeth for cutting sticks and felling small trees. They use these to dam rivers and streams, in order to create small ponds. Beavers build their homes in the middle of the ponds, where they are safe from attack.

Rocky Mountains

The Rocky Mountains stretch from Alaska to Mexico. Each part of the Rockies is like a different world, with snow-covered peaks, summer meadows grazed by goats, and forested lower slopes, where grizzly and black bears roam.

Internet link
For a link to a website where you can listen to bear sounds and see video clips of bears, go to
www.usborne-quicklinks.com

A bald eagle soars in the air on its wide wings. Bald eagles are named for the white feathers on their heads, as bald is an old English word for white.

Grasping talons

Bald eagles live near rivers and lakes in the Rockies, as their main prey is fish, which they snatch from the water with their hook-like talons. As soon as an eagle catches a fish, its talons lock around it, and can only be opened again when the eagle pushes down on a hard surface. This stops the fish from slipping from its grasp.

Hoofing it

Rocky Mountain goats are the only large mammals nimble enough to survive on the highest peaks. The inner pads on their hooves are soft and curved, providing a suction-like grip on steep rocks.

Both males and females have sharp horns. Males use them to fight during the mating season, when they stand beside each other and try to stab each other's flanks.

This Rocky Mountain goat is making a steep descent. Mountain goats are so well adapted to climbing that they rarely fall.

46

Bears in trees

Black bears have short, tightly curved claws, which are perfect for climbing trees. They rely on their climbing abilities to escape from danger, and one of the first things a mother bear does is teach her cubs to climb. Black bears also climb trees in search of nuts, fruit and bees' nests, so they can get at the honey, which they love.

These black bear cubs feel safe high up in a tree. They climb by digging their front claws into the bark, then pushing themselves up with their back paws.

47

The prairies

Huge grasslands known as prairies once stretched across the USA. They were home to herds of bison and packs of wolves. Most of the prairie land is now used for farming. The bison and wolves are almost gone, but many small animals live in the patches of prairie that remain.

Internet link

For a link to a website where you can explore a virtual prairie dog city, go to **www.usborne-quicklinks.com**

Owl burrows

There are no trees on the prairies, so birds have to adapt to life on the ground. Burrowing owls nest and sleep in underground burrows. They have many enemies, including foxes and ferrets, which they scare off by making hissing noises so they sound like snakes.

This baby burrowing owl is fluffing its feathers to get rid of dust from its burrow.

Booming sounds

On spring mornings, the prairies are filled with the booming sounds of prairie chickens, as males gather together to attract females. They make the noise by puffing out air sacs on their necks and only stop when they have attracted a mate.

Male prairie chickens inflate their orange air sacs, fan their tail feathers and drum their feet to attract females.

Top dogs

The main predators on the prairies are coyotes, one of the fastest members of the dog family. They are very noisy animals. The leader in a pack controls the others with threatening barks. At night coyote howls travel miles across the prairies, as packs call to each other to mark their territories.

This coyote fight may look vicious, but the coyotes are only play fighting. This helps them to develop their hunting skills.

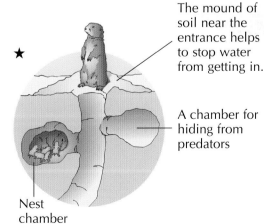

The mound of soil near the entrance helps to stop water from getting in.

A chamber for hiding from predators

Nest chamber

This shows part of a tunnel within a prairie dog city. The mound on top of the tunnel is also used as a lookout. Prairie dogs whistle if there is danger, to warn others to hide underground.

Secret tunnels

Underneath the prairies are huge networks of tunnels. These are made by prairie dogs, which are actually a type of burrowing squirrel. The tunnels, known as prairie dog cities, have many different chambers. There are nest chambers for sleeping, toilet chambers and storage chambers, where seeds are stored ready for winter.

Sonoran Desert

The Sonoran is the hottest desert in North America, but over 2,000 species of plants and over 500 species of animals live there. There is so much wildlife in the Sonoran as it has two rainy seasons, with light rains in winter and heavy downpours in summer.

Cool burrows

Kangaroo rats are small rodents that hop on their back legs like kangaroos. They avoid the day's heat by sheltering in burrows, sealing up the entrance to stop moisture from their breath from escaping. This helps the air in the burrow stay cool.

★

Kangaroo rats seal up their burrows by kicking dirt into the entrance.

You can see the blood vessels in this jackrabbit's huge ears. These help it to keep cool.

Big ears

Some animals in the Sonoran use their ears to keep cool. Kit foxes and jackrabbits have large, thin ears, filled with blood vessels. As breezes blow over their ears, their blood is cooled and then circulated around the body.

Here you can see the Sonoran Desert at sunset. The big cacti are saguaros.

Desert giants

The Sonoran is home to the USA's largest cactus – the saguaro. Over a lifetime of around 150 years, saguaros can grow up to 15m (50ft) high. They provide shelter for birds such as the gilded flicker, which makes nest holes in the stems and branches. When the birds leave, the nests are taken over by insects, lizards and elf owls.

Poisonous monster

There are only two poisonous lizards in the world and one of them, the gila monster, lives in the Sonoran. It grabs its prey in a vice-like bite, then poison from its lower jaw flows into its victim through grooves in its teeth.

Internet link

For a link to a website where you can watch a short movie on how animals battle for survival in the world's deserts, go to www.usborne-quicklinks.com

This gila monster is basking on the warm sand. You can see its short, sharp claws, which it uses for digging shelters in the sand.

Florida Everglades

The swamps of the Everglades cover the southern tip of Florida. The area has a dazzling variety of water birds, as well as a number of poisonous snakes and rare mammals. It is also the only place in the world where alligators and crocodiles live side by side.

The fourth tooth in the lower jaw of a crocodile can always be seen, even when it shuts its mouth.

An alligator's fourth tooth fits into a socket, so it can't be seen when it closes its mouth.

★

These side views show how to tell the difference between crocodiles and alligators.

Endless teeth

Alligators are the largest predators in the Everglades. They can grow up to 6m (20ft) long and have huge mouths filled with around 80 sharp teeth. As their teeth wear down, they are replaced by new ones. An alligator can go through 3,000 teeth in a lifetime.

Gator holes

Alligators like to keep wet, but in winter, much of the Everglades dries up. So alligators dig holes in the mud, known as gator holes, which fill up with water seeping in from underground. Fish, turtles and frogs collect in the holes. Many of these animals are eaten by the hungry alligators.

An alligator peers above the water. Its nostrils are on top of its head, so it can lie almost entirely submerged in water and still breathe.

This roseate spoonbill is just taking off. Roseate spoonbills are named for their rosy pink feathers and long, spoon-shaped beaks.

Snakebirds

Snakebirds get their name from the way they swim. A snakebird keeps its body partly underwater, with just its long neck and head moving above the surface like a snake. Unlike most water birds, they don't have waterproof feathers. After diving to catch prey, they come ashore and stretch out their wings to dry their feathers in the sun.

Turning pink

Roseate spoonbills nest in trees, but at sunrise each morning they flock to shallow water, where they feel for shrimp and crabs with their sensitive beaks. Spoonbills are born white, but over time chemicals in their food turn their legs and feathers bright pink.

A snakebird dives underwater to catch a fish, which it spears on the end of its long, sharp beak.

It flips the fish into the air and swallows it head first, so the fish's scales and fins don't catch in its throat. ★

Internet link

For a link to a website with an interactive map showing where alligators and crocodiles live, go to **www.usborne-quicklinks.com**

Heat-seeking snakes

Cottonmouths can detect heat given off by other animals using heat sensors near their mouths. This means they can tell if another animal is near just by sensing a change in the temperature. They use their heat sensors to hunt for prey at night and to detect predators. They are highly aggressive, but usually give warning signals before they attack. ★

To warn off a predator, a cottonmouth opens its mouth and displays the white skin inside.

The cottonmouth also shakes its tail violently. If the predator doesn't move away, the snake may attack.

Africa

Some of the world's most spectacular wildlife lives in Africa, including gorillas, lions, elephants and giraffes. Open grasslands are scattered across the continent, tropical rainforests stretch across the middle and to the north lies the Sahara Desert, where only the very toughest animals can survive.

Soda lakes

The Great Rift Valley, in Kenya and Tanzania, is dry for most of the year, but during the rainy season shallow soda lakes appear, fed partly by the rains and partly by soda-rich springs. Many tiny creatures thrive in the lakes, and millions of flamingoes congregate to feed on them. The flamingoes are so numerous, they turn the lakes into a mass of pink.

This is a flock of greater flamingoes. Flamingoes always fly with their heads and necks stretched out, like this.

Internet link
For links to websites with fascinating facts about African animals, go to
www.usborne-quicklinks.com

Map key

Forests
Deserts
Mountains
Other (grassland, farmland & cities)

This map shows just some of the animals that live in Africa.

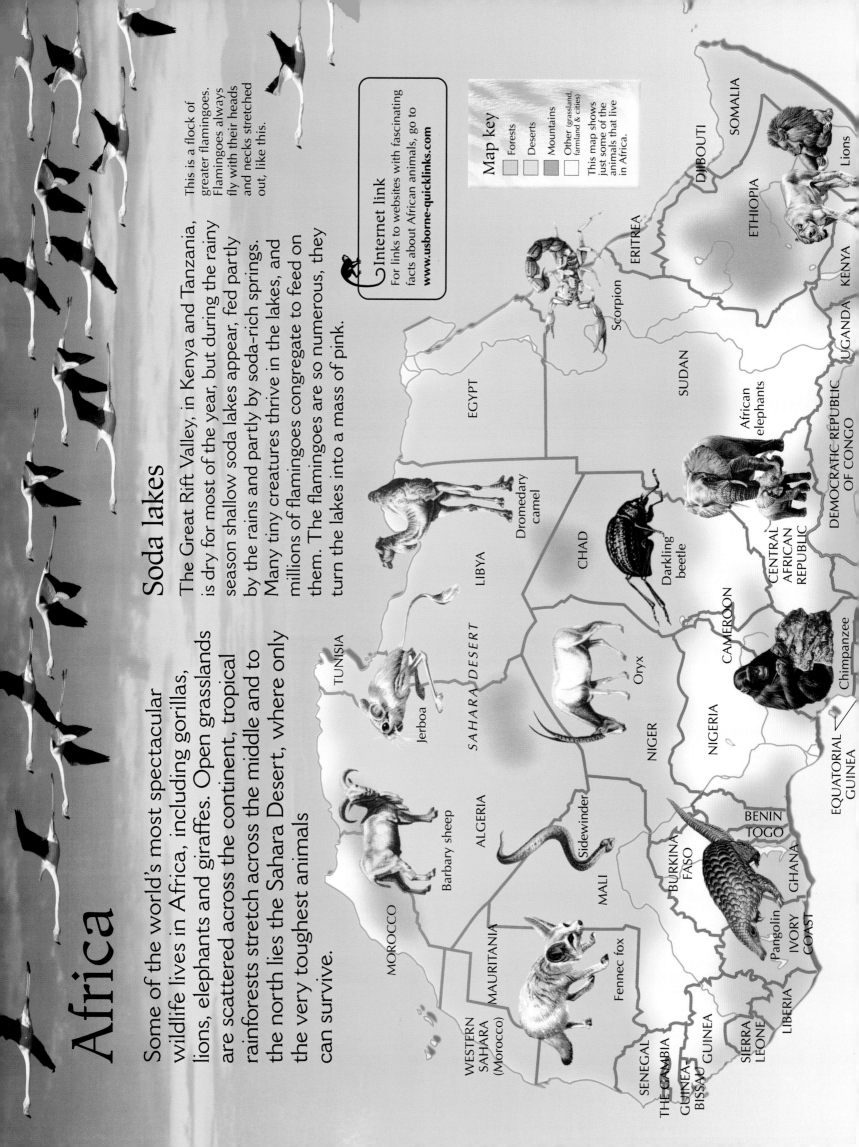

Scorpion

Dromedary camel

African elephants

Darkling beetle

Chimpanzee

Oryx

Jerboa

SAHARA DESERT

Barbary sheep

Sidewinder

Fennec fox

Pangolin

Lions

Countries

MOROCCO
WESTERN SAHARA (Morocco)
MAURITANIA
TUNISIA
ALGERIA
LIBYA
EGYPT
MALI
NIGER
CHAD
SUDAN
ERITREA
DJIBOUTI
SOMALIA
ETHIOPIA
KENYA
UGANDA
DEMOCRATIC REPUBLIC OF CONGO
CENTRAL AFRICAN REPUBLIC
CAMEROON
NIGERIA
BENIN
TOGO
BURKINA FASO
GHANA
IVORY COAST
LIBERIA
SIERRA LEONE
GUINEA
GUINEA-BISSAU
THE GAMBIA
SENEGAL
EQUATORIAL GUINEA

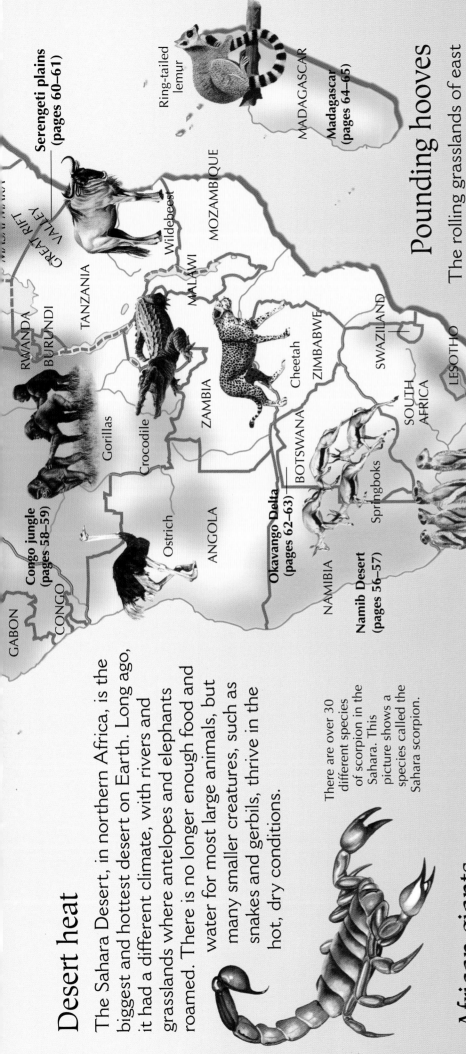

Ring-tailed lemur

MADAGASCAR

MOZAMBIQUE

Wildebeest

GREAT RIFT VALLEY

MALAWI

TANZANIA

RWANDA
BURUNDI

Gorillas

Crocodile

ZAMBIA

ZIMBABWE

Cheetah

SWAZILAND

LESOTHO

Meerkats

SOUTH
AFRICA

BOTSWANA

Springboks

Ostrich

ANGOLA

NAMIBIA

GABON
CONGO

Desert heat

The Sahara Desert, in northern Africa, is the biggest and hottest desert on Earth. Long ago, it had a different climate, with rivers and grasslands where antelopes and elephants roamed. There is no longer enough food and water for most large animals, but many smaller creatures, such as snakes and gerbils, thrive in the hot, dry conditions.

There are over 30 different species of scorpion in the Sahara. This picture shows a species called the Sahara scorpion.

African giants

There are many giants in southern Africa. Giraffes are the tallest animals, growing up to 6m (20ft) tall. Goliath beetles are one of the largest insects and ostriches are the biggest birds. But the biggest land animals of all are African elephants. Adult males are twice as tall as a person and weigh as much as five small cars.

Pounding hooves

The rolling grasslands of east Africa are the setting for one of the world's greatest wildlife spectacles – the wildebeest migration. Over 1.4 million wildebeest and 200,000 zebras and gazelles migrate thousands of miles each year, from the vast Serengeti plains to the hills of Kenya's Masai Mara, in search of fresh grass.

Even in silhouette, it's easy to recognize giraffes' distinctive shape, with their long necks and sloping shoulders.

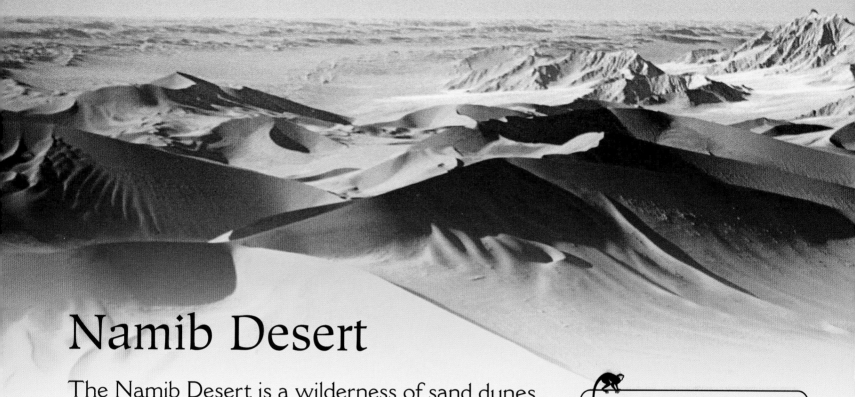

Namib Desert

The Namib Desert is a wilderness of sand dunes and barren gravel plains that stretches along the coast of southwest Africa. The animals that live in this hot, dry region have developed some unusual ways of coping with the harsh conditions.

Internet link

For a link to a website where you can play an animal matching game set in the Namib Desert, go to **www.usborne-quicklinks.com**

Dancing lizards

By day, the surface of the sand dunes can reach a baking 60°C (140°F). To avoid burning their feet on the hot sand, shovel-snouted lizards dash quickly over the dunes. Whenever they stop, they lift up two of their feet at a time. This strange-looking movement is called a thermal dance. When the heat becomes unbearable, the lizards dive headfirst into the sand, to reach the cooler sand below. They can stay buried for up to 24 hours.

This shovel-snouted lizard is doing its thermal dance. Its feet never touch the hot ground for more than a few seconds.

Desert elephants

Several dry river valleys wind across the Namib Desert. After bursts of rain, their sandy beds fill up and trees along their banks burst into leaf. This provides food and water for a small population of elephants, which wander up and down the river valleys in family groups.

Fog drinkers

As dawn begins to break, a dense fog blows into the desert from the cold Atlantic Ocean. This fog brings precious moisture to many small animals. Fog-basking beetles climb up sand dunes and angle their bodies into the wind to collect moisture droplets. In a few hours, they can collect up to 40% of their body weight in water.

Each morning, fog-basking beetles emerge from their burrows and run to the top of a sand dune.

They then turn around and do a kind of handstand, so they can drink the water droplets that run into their mouths.

Sand dune survivors

The oryx is one of the few large animals that can survive among the sand dunes. Oryxes feed on the juicy flesh of desert melons. The melon juice enables them to go for long periods without water. They can also cope with very high temperatures. Networks of fine blood vessels in their noses cool blood entering their brains, so that they don't get too hot.

All oryxes have sharp, pointed horns, like these. Oryxes can kill attacking lions by impaling them on their horns.

Congo jungle

The Congo is a huge area of dense rainforest right in the middle of Africa. It is home to an extraordinary range of animals, including great apes, such as gorillas and chimpanzees, half the elephants of Africa, giant insects and rare antelopes.

Internet link

For a link to a website where you can go on a tour of the Congo and see video clips of Congo animals, go to
www.usborne-quicklinks.com

This is a family group of mountain gorillas. Baby gorillas are extremely playful. The one on the right is lying upside down for fun.

Gentle giants

Gorillas live deep in the forest, in close family groups. Although they are large, powerful animals, gorillas are not usually aggressive, and mainly eat plants. Because of their large size, gorillas need to eat a lot of food. A typical gorilla day consists of two hours of heavy eating followed by a nap, then leisurely feeding for the rest of the afternoon.

Gorillas prefer to make threat displays rather than fight. The males beat their chests, like this, to warn off attackers.

★

Grooming monkeys

Red colobus monkeys live high up in the tree tops in groups of up to 40. They spend much of their time grooming – combing through each other's hair and removing parasites and dead skin with their lips or tongues. This keeps them healthy, and also helps to strengthen the bonds between them.

Giant bugs

Goliath beetles are among the largest and heaviest insects in the world. They can grow to around the size of your hand. Despite their large size, they fly well and feed on ripe fruit high up in the canopy. They make loud buzzing noises as they fly, making them sound like mini helicopters.

Male goliath beetles battle with each other for mates or feeding sites. They fight using the Y-shaped horns on their heads, like this.

Like all red colobus monkeys, this mother and baby have long fur on their bodies. Scientists think it may act like a parachute, slowing their fall as they leap from tree to tree.

This is a young bongo antelope (adults have much longer horns). Its large ears help it to listen out for predators.

Congo bongos

Bongo antelopes live in the densest parts of the forest. They mainly feed on low shrubs, pulling off the leaves with their long, prehensile tongues. They have also been seen eating dirt, and wood burned during lightning storms, probably for their salt content.

Serengeti plains

The Serengeti is a nature reserve in east Africa made up of rolling grasslands and scattered patches of woodland. Its name means "endless plains" in the local Masai language. The reserve protects the biggest herds of animals in Africa and has a fearsome collection of predators.

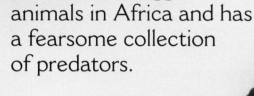
Internet link
For a link to a website where you can play a safari game taking photographs of animals on the Serengeti, go to www.usborne-quicklinks.com

Keeping cool

African elephants live in family groups, led by an adult female. Together, they travel huge distances each day in search of food. They cool down by wallowing in pools or, if water is scarce, by sucking up water in their trunks and squirting it over their bodies. After bathing, elephants cover their skin with dirt for protection from insects.

The elephants in this herd are using their trunks to drink from a water hole. The trunks are amazingly supple, with around 150,000 muscles.

Top cats

Lions are the largest and most powerful hunters in the Serengeti. They live in groups of 20 or more, known as prides, and often hunt together to increase their chances of catching prey. Females do most of the hunting, but males are usually the first to eat.

Cat naps

Leopards mostly live in patches of woodland. They lounge and nap in large trees by day and come down to hunt at night. After making a kill, they often drag the body into a tree. This keeps it out of the way of other animals, such as hyenas, that might want to steal it.

This is a classic leopard pose, with the leopard dangling its legs from a branch as it rests during the day.

Snake hunters

Secretary birds have longer legs than any other bird of prey, and grow up to 1m (3ft) high. Although they can fly, they hunt on foot, searching for lizards, insects and poisonous snakes, which they grab with their strong feet. The scales on their legs protect them from snakebites.

Secretary birds stamp their prey to death with their tough feet.

Okavango Delta

Some rivers never reach the sea. In the dry southern African country of Botswana, the Okavango River meets the sands of the Kalahari Desert. The river can go no further. It spreads out into a maze of channels and islands called the Okavango Delta. This vast wetland wilderness is a haven for wildlife.

Hippo lawns

Hippopotamuses live in the middle of the delta in small groups called pods. Their skin is very sensitive to sunlight, so they spend the daytime in the water. After dark, when it gets cooler, they come out to graze on the islands. They cut the grass close to the ground with their lips, clearing neat areas known as hippo lawns.

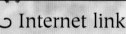

Internet link

For a link to a website where you can go on a virtual safari around the Okavango Delta, go to
www.usborne-quicklinks.com

This hippopotamus has opened its mouth to warn rivals to keep away. Hippopotamuses use their enormous front teeth to threaten and sometimes bite each other.

Water-loving lechwe

Red lechwe are antelopes that spend almost as much time in water as on land. They have long, splayed hooves to help support them on swampy ground, and will wade up to their bellies in water to reach food. They also take to water to escape from predators, such as wild dogs.

These red lechwe are fleeing across water. You can see their strangely-shaped hooves, which help them bound across waterlogged ground.

Rocking rollers

Lilac-breasted rollers swoop and dive over the Okavango, flashing their bright feathers. Rollers get their name from their impressive courtship displays – they dive quickly through the air with a side-to-side rocking motion. As they dive, they make loud, raucous "zaaak, zaaak" noises. Once rollers have found a mate, they stay together for life.

This lilac-breasted roller has raised its wings ready for flight. It will push off with its feet and make a plunge for prey on the ground.

Heron umbrella

Black herons keep to the shallow waters of the delta, where they hunt for fish. They have a cunning way of feeding, spreading their wings like an umbrella to cast a shadow over the water. Fish are attracted to the shade, but there they are easier for herons to see and catch.

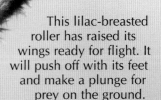

A black heron stands very still as a fish swims into the shadow cast by its wings.

It grabs the fish with its beak as soon as it comes close enough.

★

63

Madagascar

Most of Madagascar's amazing wildlife is found nowhere else on Earth. This is because Madagascar broke away from Africa over 80 million years ago. Since then, animals such as lemurs have developed in complete isolation from the rest of the world.

Hidden lizards

Leaf-tailed geckos are small lizards that live on tree trunks and use amazing camouflage to hide from predators. Their flattened bodies are the exact shade and texture of bark and they are fringed with a frill of skin that blends into the trunk, leaving no tell-tale shadow.

Giraffe-necked weevils like this one can grow about as long as your finger. The red patches are its wing cases.

If a predator gets too close to a gecko, it opens its mouth like this, to startle the predator with the bright red lining.

Leaf rolling

Giraffe-necked weevils, a kind of beetle, have longer necks than any other insect. They use their long necks to roll small leaves into tube shapes. A female weevil lays a single egg inside the tube, where it is hidden from predators until it hatches.

Dancing lemurs

Sifakas are lemurs that spend most of their time in trees, but occasionally they have to cross open ground. They then stand on their hind legs and break into a strange, sideways gallop, criss-crossing their legs in mid-air as they leap. This is the only way they can move on the ground, as their front legs are designed for climbing trees, and are too short for them to move on all fours.

Finger licking

Aye-ayes are rare, strange-looking lemurs. They feed at night, pressing their huge ears against trees to listen for grubs under the bark. Then they use their sharp teeth to bite holes in the bark, before winkling out the grubs with their long, thin middle fingers.

An aye-aye's long middle finger can reach deep into a hole to probe for grubs.

★

Puzzling bugs

Madagascar's flatid bugs have cunning disguises to help them survive. During their growing stage they can cover themselves in a waxy white substance that makes predators think they are foul to taste. As pink adults, they gather in groups to look like flowers.

This baby sifaka clings on tightly as its mother leaps across the ground. The mother is holding out her short front legs for balance.

Internet link
For a link to a website where you can watch short video clips of Madagascan animals, go to
www.usborne-quicklinks.com

Adult flatid bugs pack tightly together to look like petals on a flower.

★

Europe

Europe is a small continent and over 700 million people live there, leaving little room for wildlife. The animals are not as varied as on other continents, but are just as fascinating. The most successful animals are those that have learned to survive alongside humans.

Going wild

Many of Europe's animals have been domesticated, which means they have been bred by humans so they can be used for meat, wool or transportation. But in the Camargue, in France, the reverse has happened. Some Camargue horses, which are descended from domesticated horses, have been returned to the wild. The horses roam freely around the countryside in small herds.

These are Camargue horses, small white horses that live in the wild in the marshlands of southern France.

The Western Isles (pages 72–73)

Puffin

Badger

UNITED KINGDOM

IRELAND

Fallow deer

Grey seal

DENMARK

Barn owls

NETHERLANDS

GERMANY

Wolverine

Northern lynx

SWEDEN

FINLAN

NORWAY

Reindeer

RUSSIA

Wild boars

POLAND

CZECH REPUBLIC

SLOVAK

Kingfisher

BELGIUM

Red fox

Hedgehog

Ibex

FRANCE

SWITZERLAND

AUSTRIA

HUNGAR

Chamois

SLOVENIA

CROATIA

Bearded vulture

Pyrenees Mountains (pages 68–69)

THE CAMARGUE

BOSNIA AND HERZEGOVINA

ITALY

Tiger salamander

ALBAN

PORTUGAL

SPAIN

Coto Doñana (pages 70–71)

Striped dolphin

Yellow-bellied toad

Wallcreeper

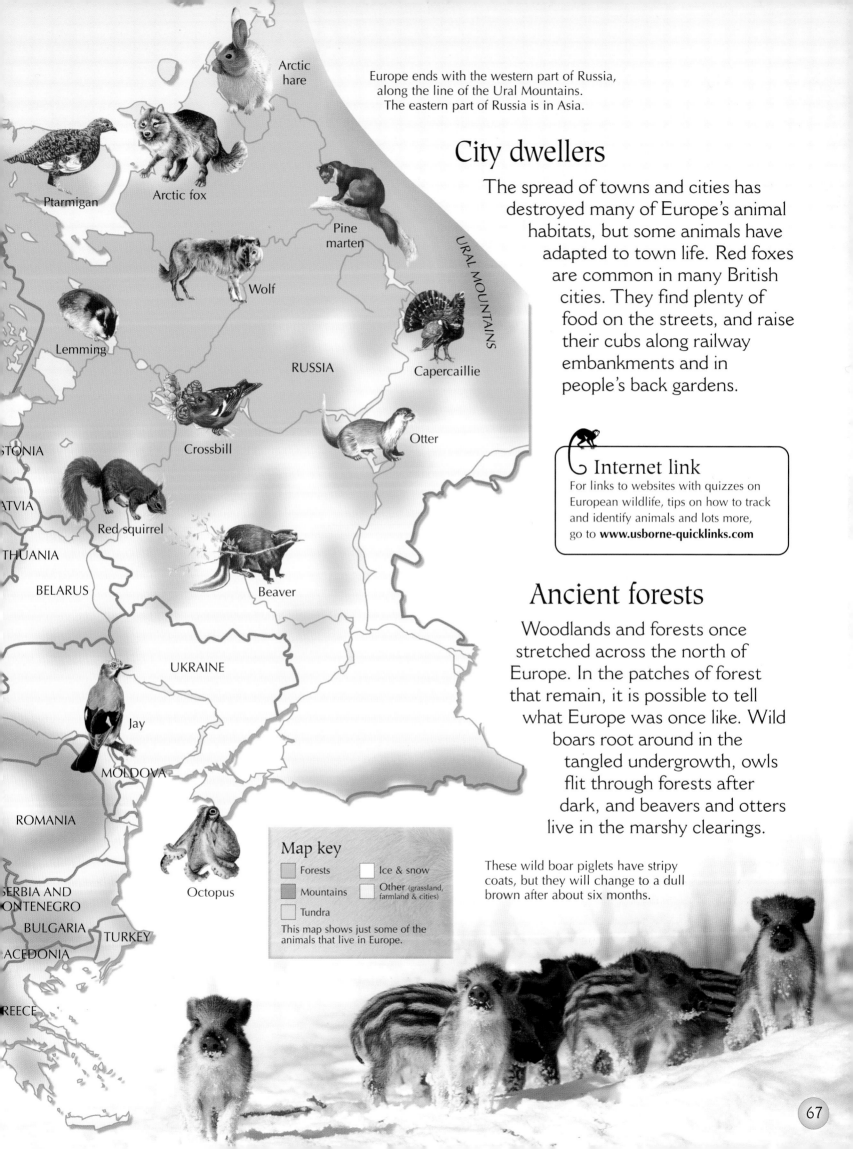

Arctic hare

Ptarmigan

Arctic fox

Pine marten

URAL MOUNTAINS

Wolf

Lemming

RUSSIA

Capercaillie

Crossbill

Otter

STONIA

ATVIA

Red squirrel

THUANIA

BELARUS

Beaver

UKRAINE

Jay

MOLDOVA

ROMANIA

Octopus

SERBIA AND
ONTENEGRO

BULGARIA

TURKEY

ACEDONIA

REECE

Europe ends with the western part of Russia,
along the line of the Ural Mountains.
The eastern part of Russia is in Asia.

City dwellers

The spread of towns and cities has destroyed many of Europe's animal habitats, but some animals have adapted to town life. Red foxes are common in many British cities. They find plenty of food on the streets, and raise their cubs along railway embankments and in people's back gardens.

Internet link

For links to websites with quizzes on European wildlife, tips on how to track and identify animals and lots more, go to www.usborne-quicklinks.com

Ancient forests

Woodlands and forests once stretched across the north of Europe. In the patches of forest that remain, it is possible to tell what Europe was once like. Wild boars root around in the tangled undergrowth, owls flit through forests after dark, and beavers and otters live in the marshy clearings.

These wild boar piglets have stripy coats, but they will change to a dull brown after about six months.

Map key

Forests

Mountains

Tundra

Ice & snow

Other (grassland, farmland & cities)

This map shows just some of the animals that live in Europe.

Pyrenees Mountains

The rugged Pyrenees Mountains straddle the border between France and Spain. There are parts of the Pyrenees that remain as wild today as they were hundreds of years ago. Wild boars and goats roam freely, and vultures and eagles soar through the skies.

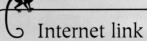
Internet link

For a link to a website where you can listen to birds and other animals in the Pyrenees, go to
www.usborne-quicklinks.com

Getting a grip

Ibexes are rare wild goats that live high up on the rocky slopes. They can climb almost vertical cliff faces, using their narrow-edged hooves to dig into cracks in the rocks. Males have long, curved horns, which they can use to scratch their backs.

The horns of these male ibexes are around 1m (3ft) long. Ibexes bow their heads and charge with their horns lowered to scare off predators, such as bears and wolves.

Winter burrows

Small mammals called marmots live in family groups on the grassy mountain meadows. They eat as much as they can during spring and summer, then hibernate for the rest of the year in burrows. The last marmot into the burrow plugs the entrance with earth to keep the warmth in and predators out.

Marmots greet each other by touching noses, so that they can smell to see if they are from the same family group.

Bone breakers

Bearded vultures fly high above the mountains on currents of warm air, looking out for carcasses. Unlike other vultures, bearded vultures feed on bones rather than flesh. They pick up the bones in their claws, then drop them onto rocks from a great height in order to smash them. The vultures then swallow the broken pieces.

Sensitive snouts

Pyrenean desmans are unusual, mole-like mammals that live in fast-flowing rivers and streams. During the day, they rest in burrows along the riverbank, but at night they come out to hunt for shrimps, crayfish and insects. They have webbed feet, which enable them to swim quickly, and sensitive hairs on their snouts so they can feel for prey.

This bearded vulture is using warm air currents, called thermals, to soar high above a valley. With its sharp eyesight, it can spot dead animals far below.

★

A Pyrenean desman disturbs the gravel on the riverbed, exposing any creatures hiding there. The long, sensitive hairs on its snout detect the pressure waves made by prey trying to escape.

Butcher birds

Shrikes are small birds that migrate to the Pyrenees each spring. They are also known as butcher birds, because of the way they impale their prey on the spikes of thorn bushes or barbed wire. This gives them a ready-made larder of food to eat from on days when they don't catch anything.

This red-backed shrike is sitting by its larder, where it has stored a butterfly and a small lizard. Shrikes don't kill their prey before impaling it, so it stays fresh for longer.

Coto Doñana

Before the Guadalquivir River reaches the sea, it splits off to form a network of channels and islands known as Coto Doñana. The area is made up of salt lakes, marshy ground and patches of woodland. It was once a royal hunting ground, but today it is Europe's largest national park.

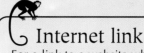
Internet link
For a link to a website where you can play games to find out more about wetland wildlife, go to www.usborne-quicklinks.com

Rare cat

Iberian lynxes prowl the Doñana woodlands at night, hunting mainly for rabbits. Lynxes drag or carry their prey until they find a safe place to eat it. On average, they need to eat a rabbit a day to stay healthy, but a fall in rabbit populations, combined with habitat loss, has made them the most endangered wild cats in the world.

Battling antlers

In September and October, the air is filled with the bellowing sounds of red deer, as males compete for female attention. Red deer live in separate male and female groups for most of the year but, during the courtship months, each stag tries to win over a group of females, and challenges any male rivals. If neither stag backs down, they bow their heads and clash their antlers in a vicious struggle.

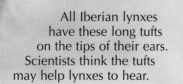

All Iberian lynxes have these long tufts on the tips of their ears. Scientists think the tufts may help lynxes to hear.

Male red deer lock their antlers as a test of strength. They fight until one stag admits defeat by moving away, or is badly injured. The winner stays with the females and gets to mate with them.

Bee-eaters

European bee-eaters are small birds that travel thousands of miles each year. They spend the winter in Africa, then flock to Doñana in spring, where they nest and lay their eggs in burrows along the sandy riverbanks. As their name suggests, bee-eaters mostly eat bees (though they eat other insects too).

A bee-eater knocks the sting (stinger) out of a bee's body by hitting it against a hard surface, such as a branch.

This bee-eater is about to snap up an insect. Bee-eaters usually eat up to 250 insects a day.

Upside-down eating

Flamingoes feed on tiny animals and plants in the Doñana marshes. They sweep their beaks, upside down, through the muddy water and suck in a mixture of water, mud and food. The food sticks to ridges inside their beaks. They then push out the mud and water with their tongues, and swallow their food.

These greater flamingoes are searching for small animals in the mud, which they disturb from the bottom by treading with their webbed feet.

The Western Isles

Lying at the northwest edge of Europe, the Western Isles, or Hebrides, are a chain of wild and windswept islands that stretch over 390km (150 miles) across the Atlantic Ocean. Many seabirds nest along the steep cliffs, while sharks, seals and dolphins swim in the sheltered bays.

This is a grey seal. Its body is rounded, as it has a thick layer of insulating blubber under its skin. This enables it to survive in cold water temperatures that would kill a human within minutes.

Seals and pups

Grey seals spend most of the year at sea, but come ashore around October to breed. The babies, or pups, are born with a covering of long, creamy-white fur called lanugo, which keeps them warm. They fatten quickly on their mothers' rich milk and by three weeks old have a thick covering of blubber, and are able to shed their coats.

Surfing the waves

Common dolphins fish the waters further from the shore. They are very playful and often make fantastic somersaults out of the water. They also "bow-ride"– surfing the waves in front of fast-moving boats. The dolphins are pushed forward by pressure from the waves, so they travel faster than if they were just swimming along.

When bow-riding, a dolphin positions its body in front of the crest of the wave, so that the wave pushes it through the water.

Flocking puffins

Puffins spend the winter months floating on the open ocean and diving for fish. They are excellent swimmers, using their wings to "fly" underwater. From mid-April to May, hundreds of thousands of them flock to the Hebrides to breed.

Puffins nest on grassy cliff slopes, either in old rabbit burrows, or burrows they scratch out themselves with the sharp claws on their feet. Puffin pairs split up during the winter, but they meet again at the same burrow each spring.

All puffins have large webbed feet, like these. They use them like brakes when coming in to land, splaying them out to slow themselves down.

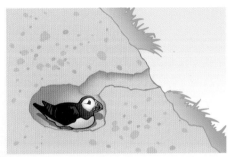

This shows a puffin inside its burrow. Each year, the female lays one egg in a chamber at the end of a narrow tunnel.

★

Speedy swimmers

The Hebrides is one of the best places in Europe to spot an otter. Otters are fast and fluid, both in and out of water. They can run as fast as a person, and they swim gracefully, powering themselves along with their strong, short legs and using their tails as rudders.

Otters are also skilful hunters. They learn from an early age, with mother otters bringing back fish and crabs for their cubs to play with, so the cubs can develop their hunting skills.

This is a family of otters. Although they look wet from the water, their outer hairs are water-repellent, keeping their thick undercoats warm and dry.

Internet link
For a link to a website where you can watch fantastic video clips of puffins, go to **www.usborne-quicklinks.com**

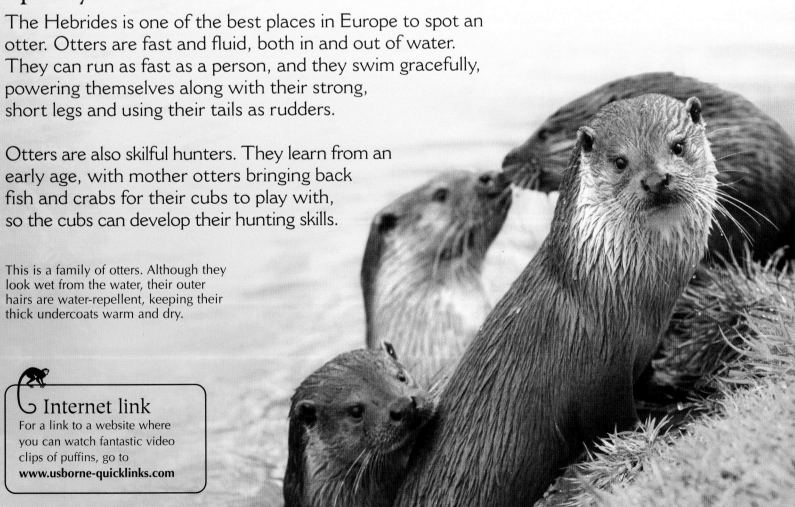

Asia

Asia is the largest continent in the world. Bands of forest, grassland and desert sweep across the north and central regions. To the south lies a different world: India, and the tropical forests of the southeast.

These are Japanese cranes, symbols of luck in Japan.

Wild horses

A corridor of grassland known as steppe stretches across central Asia. The Mongolian steppe is home to the last herds of truly wild horses, called takhi, which have never been domesticated. Takhi are smaller than domestic horses and have upright manes.

Crossing continents

India is separated from the rest of Asia by the world's highest mountain range – the Himalayas. There are few passable land routes through the Himalayas, but many animals have still spread between the rest of the world and India. Elephants came to India from Africa, and tigers from Siberia. India also has many native animals of its own.

RUSSIA

Wolf

Wolverine

KAZAKHSTAN

Saiga antelope

GEORGIA

TURKEY

ARMENIA

AZERBAIJAN

UZBEKISTAN

TURKMENISTAN

KYRGYZSTAN

TAJIKISTAN

Yak

CYPRUS

LEBANON   SYRIA

ISRAEL

JORDAN

IRAQ

IRAN

AFGHANISTAN

Himalayan Mountains (pages 78–79)

Griffon vulture

PAKISTAN

KUWAIT

Caracal

Southwestern deserts (pages 76–77)

Asian elephants

NEPAL

King cobra

SAUDI ARABIA

Dromedary camel

INDIA

OMAN

YEMEN

Reef shark

Bengal tiger

SRI LANKA

This is a gharial, a crocodile-like animal found only in rivers in northern India and Nepal. Gharials swish their long slender snouts from side to side in the water to catch fish.

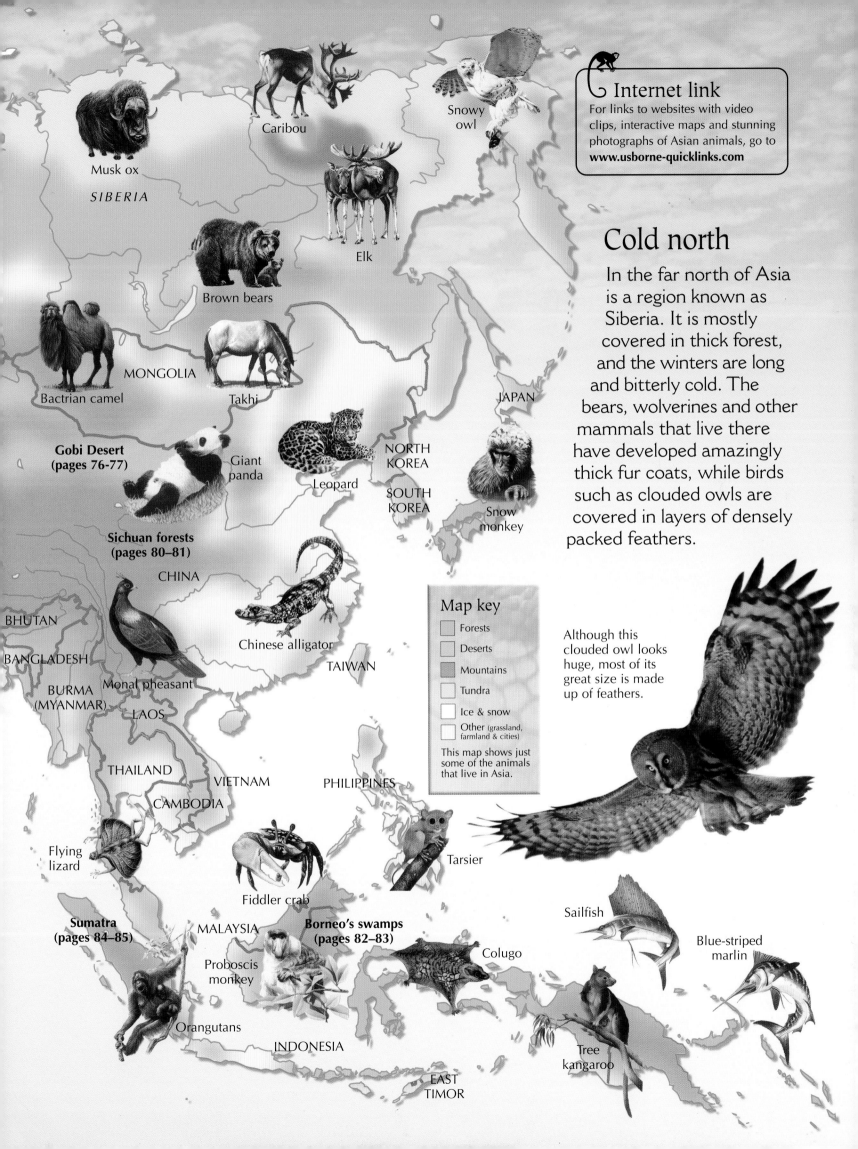

Caribou

Musk ox

SIBERIA

Snowy
owl

Elk

Brown bears

Bactrian camel

MONGOLIA

Takhi

JAPAN

**Gobi Desert
(pages 76-77)**

Giant
panda

Leopard

NORTH
KOREA

SOUTH
KOREA

Snow
monkey

**Sichuan forests
(pages 80–81)**

CHINA

Chinese alligator

BHUTAN

BANGLADESH

Monal pheasant

BURMA
(MYANMAR)

LAOS

TAIWAN

THAILAND

VIETNAM

CAMBODIA

PHILIPPINES

Flying
lizard

Fiddler crab

Tarsier

**Sumatra
(pages 84–85)**

MALAYSIA

**Borneo's swamps
(pages 82–83)**

Proboscis
monkey

Colugo

Sailfish

Blue-striped
marlin

Orangutans

INDONESIA

Tree
kangaroo

EAST
TIMOR

Internet link
For links to websites with video
clips, interactive maps and stunning
photographs of Asian animals, go to
www.usborne-quicklinks.com

Cold north

In the far north of Asia
is a region known as
Siberia. It is mostly
covered in thick forest,
and the winters are long
and bitterly cold. The
bears, wolverines and other
mammals that live there
have developed amazingly
thick fur coats, while birds
such as clouded owls are
covered in layers of densely
packed feathers.

Although this
clouded owl looks
huge, most of its
great size is made
up of feathers.

Map key

Forests

Deserts

Mountains

Tundra

Ice & snow

Other (grassland,
farmland & cities)

This map shows just
some of the animals
that live in Asia.

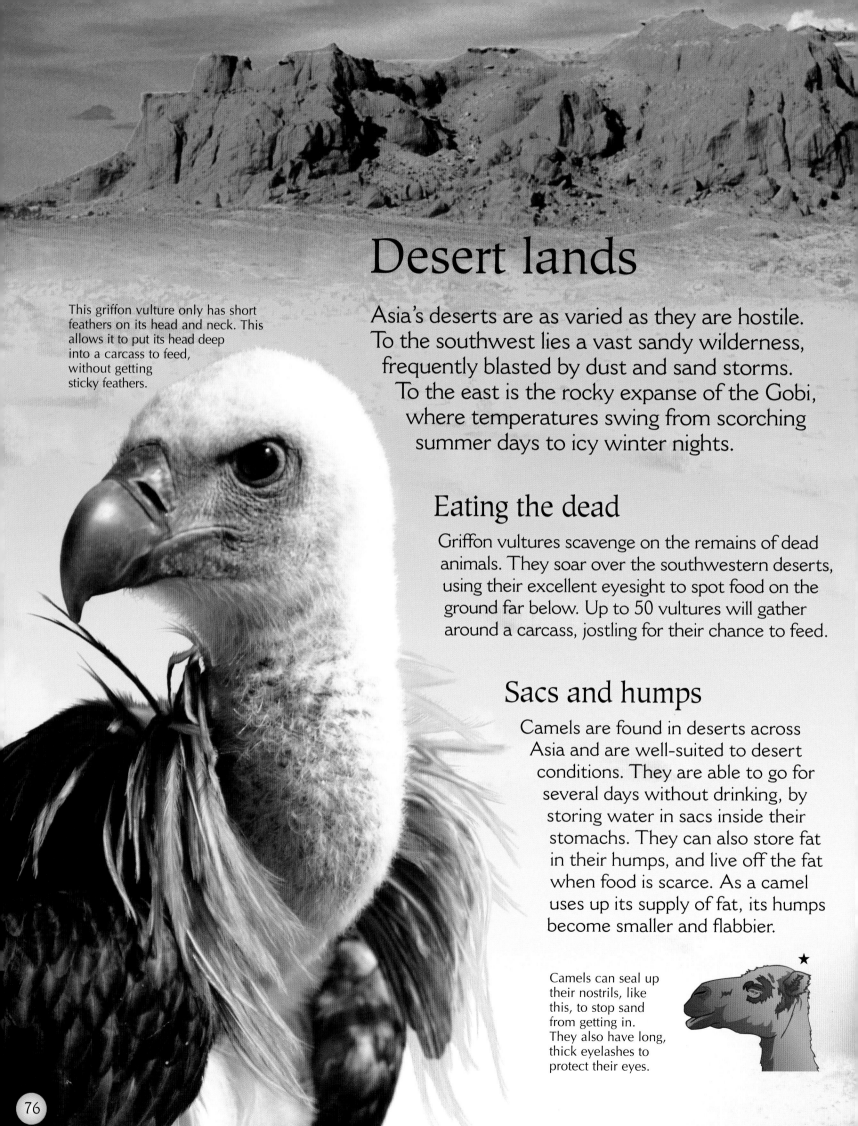

Desert lands

Asia's deserts are as varied as they are hostile. To the southwest lies a vast sandy wilderness, frequently blasted by dust and sand storms. To the east is the rocky expanse of the Gobi, where temperatures swing from scorching summer days to icy winter nights.

This griffon vulture only has short feathers on its head and neck. This allows it to put its head deep into a carcass to feed, without getting sticky feathers.

Eating the dead

Griffon vultures scavenge on the remains of dead animals. They soar over the southwestern deserts, using their excellent eyesight to spot food on the ground far below. Up to 50 vultures will gather around a carcass, jostling for their chance to feed.

Sacs and humps

Camels are found in deserts across Asia and are well-suited to desert conditions. They are able to go for several days without drinking, by storing water in sacs inside their stomachs. They can also store fat in their humps, and live off the fat when food is scarce. As a camel uses up its supply of fat, its humps become smaller and flabbier.

Camels can seal up their nostrils, like this, to stop sand from getting in. They also have long, thick eyelashes to protect their eyes.

All caracals have long black tufts on their ears. The name caracal means "black-eared" in Turkish.

These rocky outcrops are in the Gobi Desert.

Bird-catching cats

Caracals hunt for live prey in the desert, and need to be fast, agile and powerful in order to survive. They are known for their ability to catch birds, leaping high into the air to knock them down with their front paws.

Internet link

For a link to a website where you can find out about different kinds of deserts and how they formed, go to **www.usborne-quicklinks.com**

This is a long-eared desert hedgehog. Its large ears help it to lose heat, enabling it to cope with the soaring desert temperatures.

Spiky mammals

Hedgehogs and spiny mice have an advantage over other small mammals in the desert, as their spiky coats help them to ward off predators. Hedgehogs can curl up into tight balls, so their spikes stand out in every direction, forcing most attackers to leave them alone. Predators avoid spiny mice, as their sharp spines would stick in their throat.

A spiny mouse can also escape from predators by breaking off its tail. The tail doesn't grow back, but the mouse can survive without it.

★

Himalayan Mountains

The Himalayas are the highest mountains in the world. Few animals can survive on the tallest peaks – a place of freezing winds, black rock, ice and snow. Life becomes more plentiful the further down the slopes you go.

Mountain goats

Markhors are the largest kind of wild goat. In summer, they graze on grass, but in winter, they browse on leaves, often standing on their hind legs or even climbing trees to reach the juiciest leaves. Males have amazing spiralling horns, which they use to battle for females. They lock horns, then push and twist, to try to make the other goat lose its balance.

All male markhors have these spiralling horns. They can grow to over 1.5m (5ft) long.

Scaly mammals

The foothills of the Himalayas are home to pangolins – unusual mammals that are covered in scales. Baby pangolins are born with soft scales and rely totally on their mothers for protection. If a mother senses danger, she rolls into a ball, hiding the baby inside her curled-up body.

★

At first, young pangolins can't walk far, so they ride on their mothers' tails, like this.

Internet link

For a link to a website with a fun quiz about Himalayan animals, go to **www.usborne-quicklinks.com**

Snow stalkers

Snow leopards are hardly ever seen by humans. They live high up in the mountains and are now very rare, as they are hunted for their beautiful fur coats. They prey on sheep and goats, stalking their victims and then pouncing on them from above.

A snow leopard uses its powerful back legs to spring down onto unsuspecting prey.

Tiny survivors

The highest peaks of the Himalayas are permanently covered in snow. Only tiny bugs can survive there. It is too cold for plants to grow, so food is very scarce. The bugs have to rely on pollen and seeds swept up from the plains by currents of air.

A snow leopard races through the snow, with its thick, furry tail raised for balance. When resting, snow leopards wrap their tails around themselves for warmth.

Sichuan forests

The steep slopes of the Sichuan mountains are covered in thick forests and shrouded in mist. Living in the forests are more pheasant species than are found anywhere else in the world. There are also red pandas, golden monkeys and the famous giant pandas.

Internet link

For a link to a website with a live panda webcam, as well as pre-recorded video clips of pandas, go to
www.usborne-quicklinks.com

Bamboo munchers

Giant pandas live in the cloud forests at around 2,000m (6,500ft), feeding almost exclusively on bamboo shoots. Because bamboo is so low in nutrients, they have to spend up to 15 hours a day eating. They hold the bamboo in their forepaws, and have developed extra pads on their paws to help them grip the stems.

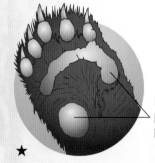

Extra paw pads

★ Here you can see the extra pads on a giant panda's forepaw.

This giant panda is munching on a bamboo stalk. Because giant pandas spend so much time eating, they always eat either sitting or lying down, to save energy.

Sleepy days

Red pandas, like giant pandas, mainly eat bamboo – around 200,000 leaves a day. They cope with their low-energy diet by spending most of the day asleep in trees. They are active only at dawn and dusk, when they come down to the forest floor to feed.

A red panda sleeps with its head tucked into its chest and its tail over its head, in order to keep warm.

★

This is an adult red panda. With its ringed tail and small size it looks more like a raccoon than a giant panda – which isn't surprising, as red pandas are actually a kind of raccoon.

Blue-faced monkeys

There are four species of golden monkeys, but Sichuan golden monkeys are the only ones with blue faces. In summer, they live in groups of up to 600 – larger groups than almost any other kind of monkey. But when cold weather sets in, they break up into smaller groups of around 60, probably because there is less food to go around.

This golden monkey is hugging her baby. Mothers are very affectionate with their children and spend hours hugging them.

Borneo's swamps

Borneo is the largest in a chain of islands in Southeast Asia. Along its coast, thick mangrove swamps provide homes for some extraordinary animals, including water-squirting fish, big-nosed monkeys and fish that can live out of water.

Tangled trees

Mangroves are trees that grow along tropical coastlines. They have stilt-like roots that reach down into the water. Saltwater kills most tree roots, but mangroves thrive in it.

Mangrove trees have bundles of roots anchoring them into muddy ground.

Young fish use the roots to hide from predators that are too big to squeeze through the gaps.

Big noses

Unique to the mangroves of Borneo are proboscis monkeys. The males have larger noses than any other monkey and the larger their noses, the more attractive they are to females. Their noses grow throughout their lives, often becoming so big that males have to push them aside to eat.

These pictures show the size of a proboscis monkey's nose at different stages of its life.

Four-month-old monkey

Five-year-old monkey

Fifteen-year-old monkey

This male proboscis monkey is munching on leaves, which are its main food. Mangrove leaves are hard to digest, so proboscis monkeys have extra chambers in their stomachs to help break down the leaves. This gives them a pot-bellied appearance.

Crab grabbers

Tarsiers are small mammals that leap through the mangrove trees at night, using their enormous eyes to see in the dark. They feed on crabs, grabbing their prey in their strong hands and then biting through the shell with their needle-sharp teeth. They shut their eyes as they bite to protect them from injury.

The swellings on the end of this tarsier's fingers act like suction cups, helping it to grip onto the tree.

Water pistol fish

Archer fish hunt for insects in the vegetation overhanging the swamps. By shooting jets of water from their mouths, they knock insects into the water. They then quickly snap up their stunned victims.

To shoot out a strong jet of water, an archer fish positions its snout just under the water's surface.

Internet link

For a link to a website where you can watch a slideshow of proboscis monkeys, go to **www.usborne-quicklinks.com**

This mudskipper is using its fins to stand. Its large eyes can focus both above and below water.

Fish out of water

Mudskippers are fish that spend most of their lives out of water. They get their name from the way they skip across the mud by flicking their muscular tails and propping themselves up on their front pair of fins. In some species, the second pair of fins forms a sucker under the body, which enables them to climb up branches and tree roots in search of food.

Sumatra

One of the largest Indonesian islands, Sumatra has some of the world's most spectacular rainforest. Plants flourish in the heavy rain, the trees are thick with chattering birds and rarely-seen mammals slink through the undergrowth.

Swinging apes

It is rare for orangutans ever to touch the ground. These great apes are superbly adapted to life in trees, with their hand-like feet and long, strong arms. Orangutans learn their way around the forest from their mothers. By the age of ten, an orangutan knows where the best fruit trees are in the forest and when each is due to bear fruit.

Orangutans don't jump from tree to tree, but swing between branches, like this.

Walled in

Rhinoceros hornbills have very unusual nesting habits. Males wall females into holes in trees by filling the opening with mud. This protects the females and young from predators, such as snakes and lizards. When the young hatch the female breaks out, but seals the nest entrance again until the young are ready to leave.

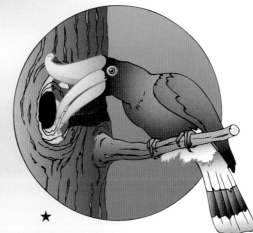

★
A male rhinoceros hornbill gradually fills up the nest hole with mud, which he carries in his beak.

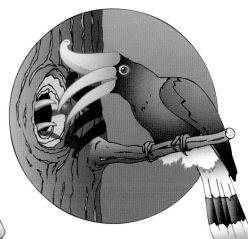

He leaves a gap in the mud, through which he passes food to his mate.

Internet link

For a link to a website where you can watch amazing video clips of orangutans, go to
www.usborne-quicklinks.com

Hairy and rare

Some incredibly rare mammals live in the Sumatran jungle. These include two-horned Sumatran rhinoceroses, which have coats of sparse, shaggy hair, and Sumatran tigers, the smallest kind of tiger. They both live in the densest part of the forest, so are hardly ever seen by humans.

Giant flower

Down on the forest floor, there are around 40,000 species of plants. One of these, the rafflesia, has the largest flower in the world, measuring up to 1m (3ft) across. It gives off a stench of rotting meat in order to attract flies to pollinate it.

This is a rafflesia flower. It only lasts for a few days, then rots into black slime.

A rare Sumatran tiger peers through the undergrowth. There are only around 400 left in the wild.

Australasia

Australasia is made up of Australia, New Guinea and New Zealand. It has been separated from the rest of the world for millions of years, and many of the animals that live there are found nowhere else on Earth.

Babies in pouches

Australia and New Guinea are home to a unique group of mammals called marsupials, which includes kangaroos and koalas. As soon as a marsupial is born, it crawls into a pouch of skin on its mother's tummy. The baby will stay inside the pouch for the first few months of its life, feeding on milk, which it sucks through its mother's teat.

Monotreme mammals

Egg-laying mammals are called monotremes and are found only in Australia and New Guinea. There are three kinds – duckbilled platypuses, short-beaked echidnas and long-beaked echidnas. Unlike other mammals, monotremes do not have any teats. Instead, baby monotremes lick up milk that seeps out of glands in the mother's skin.

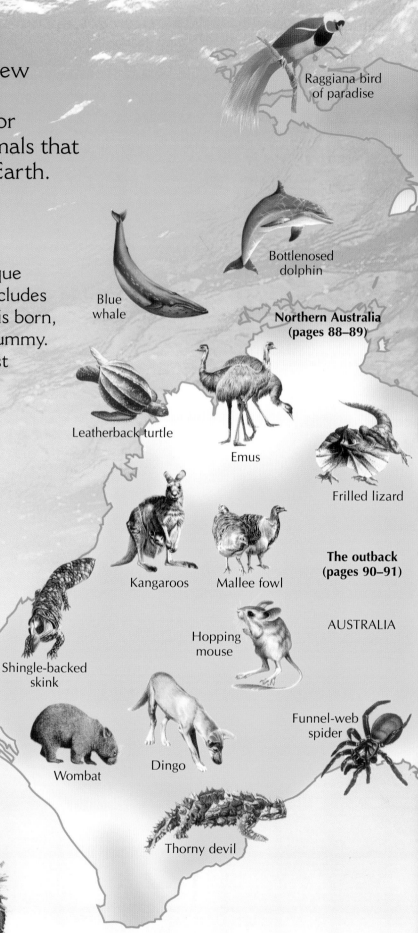

Raggiana bird of paradise

Bottlenosed dolphin

Blue whale

Northern Australia (pages 88–89)

Leatherback turtle

Emus

Frilled lizard

Kangaroos

Mallee fowl

The outback (pages 90–91)

AUSTRALIA

Shingle-backed skink

Hopping mouse

Funnel-web spider

Wombat

Dingo

Thorny devil

This is a long-beaked echidna. It is protected by a covering of spines. If you look closely, you can see that it also has hair growing between the spines.

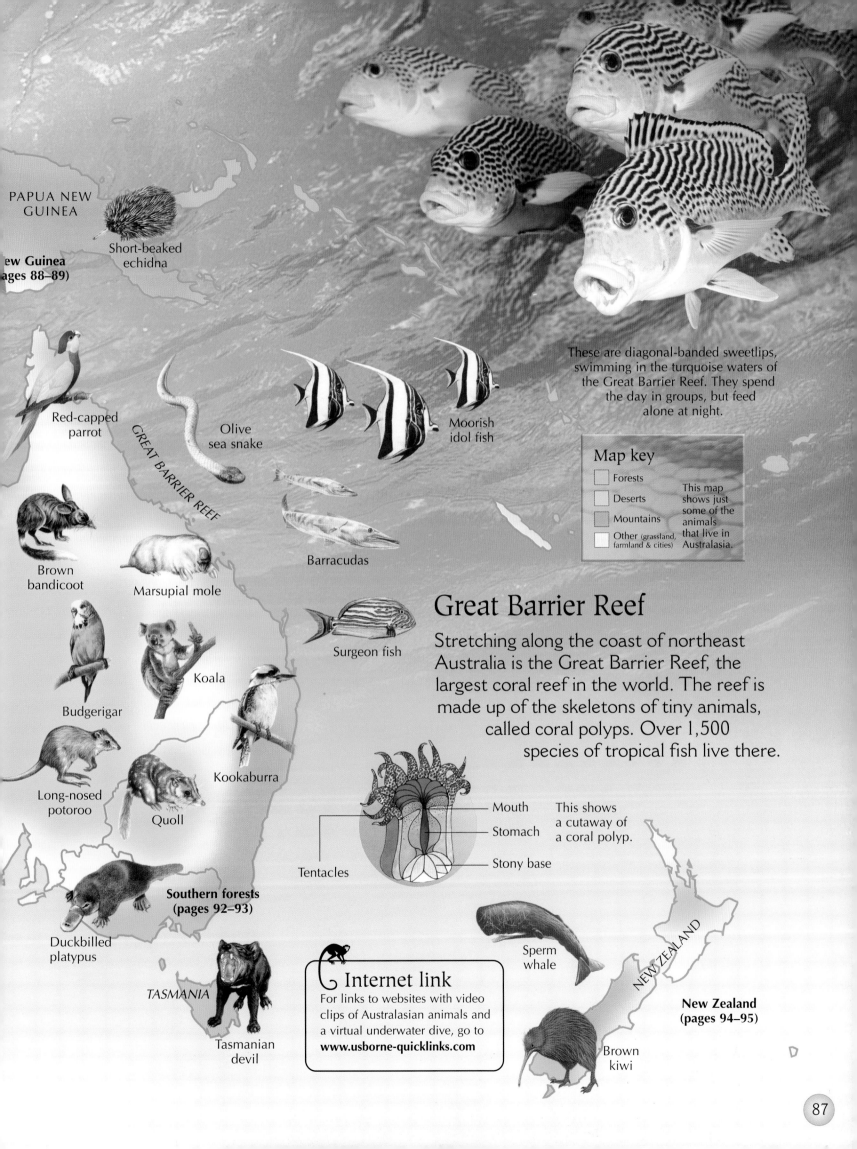

PAPUA NEW GUINEA

Short-beaked echidna

New Guinea (pages 88–89)

Red-capped parrot

GREAT BARRIER REEF

Olive sea snake

Moorish idol fish

Barracudas

Brown bandicoot

Marsupial mole

Surgeon fish

Budgerigar

Koala

Kookaburra

Long-nosed potoroo

Quoll

Duckbilled platypus

Southern forests (pages 92–93)

TASMANIA

Tasmanian devil

Sperm whale

Brown kiwi

New Zealand (pages 94–95)

NEW ZEALAND

These are diagonal-banded sweetlips, swimming in the turquoise waters of the Great Barrier Reef. They spend the day in groups, but feed alone at night.

Map key

☐ Forests
☐ Deserts
▨ Mountains
☐ Other (grassland, farmland & cities)

This map shows just some of the animals that live in Australasia.

Great Barrier Reef

Stretching along the coast of northeast Australia is the Great Barrier Reef, the largest coral reef in the world. The reef is made up of the skeletons of tiny animals, called coral polyps. Over 1,500 species of tropical fish live there.

Mouth

Stomach

Stony base

Tentacles

This shows a cutaway of a coral polyp.

Internet link

For links to websites with video clips of Australasian animals and a virtual underwater dive, go to **www.usborne-quicklinks.com**

Tropical north

The north coast of Australia and the nearby mountainous island of New Guinea are covered in lush tropical rainforest. These forests are home to over 80 species of unique mammals, including kangaroos that can climb trees, as well as many strange and beautiful birds.

Internet link

For a link to a website where you can see video clips of bird of paradise chicks being fed, go to www.usborne-quicklinks.com

This magnificent bird of paradise uses his gorgeous feathers for an eye-catching courtship display. He bobs up and down, dances and chirrups to draw the female's attention to them.

Feather displays

Birds of paradise are found only in New Guinea. The dazzling males attract the duller females by giving spectacular displays. One species, the magnificent bird of paradise, has a cloak of red and gold feathers. Males first choose a branch to display from, then strip away the leaves so their displays are easy to see. Only then do they begin to fan and shake their beautiful plumes.

You can just see the female magnificent bird of paradise on the left. Males and females only ever come together during the spring courting time.

Climbing kangaroos

Unlike kangaroos on the ground, tree kangaroos have strong front legs, and can move their back legs one at a time, which they need to do for climbing. Tree kangaroos can also hop, to get from tree to tree or down to the ground.

This Huon's tree kangaroo is gripping the tree trunk firmly with its claws, so it can look around for food.

Giant birds

Deep in the rainforest there are no large mammals. The giant of the jungle is a huge, flightless bird called the cassowary. It can run at speeds of up to 50kph (30mph) and defends itself by kicking with its big feet.

The cassowary has a bony helmet on its head, which allows it to run through thick vegetation without being injured.

★

Master builders

Male bowerbirds do not have gorgeous plumage like birds of paradise. Instead, they attract females by building complicated structures called bowers. Some species build a bower around a central stick, with a garden of moss in front. Others build bowers shaped more like tunnels or avenues. When a male has completed his bower, he attracts a female to inspect his handiwork. Females select the male whose bower impresses them most.

★

Male satin bowerbirds often decorate their bowers with feathers, like this, or with flowers and berries.

89

The outback

The central part of Australia, known as the outback, is dry and dusty, with a brief rainy season when the earth turns to mud. By day, this harsh landscape seems deserted, as animals shelter from the hot sun, but it comes alive at night.

Internet link

For a link to a website where you can do quizzes and see video clips of Australian animals, go to **www.usborne-quicklinks.com**

Leaps and bounds

Kangaroos are the largest and fastest marsupials. They bound along in two-footed leaps, using their big feet and strong back legs. Their long, muscular tails help them to balance while moving. Mothers are easily able to hop with young in their pouches, often with the baby kangaroo, or joey, peering out. Joeys can hop around from the age of three months, but return to the pouch whenever they are frightened.

★ A baby kangaroo dives into its mother's pouch headfirst. It does a somersault, then turns around so it's looking out of the pouch.

These male kangaroos are fighting each other, or boxing, in order to win the right to mate with a female. The one on the right is using its tail to prop itself up, so it can kick with its hind feet.

Nectar larders

There are ants in the outback that have developed amazing ways of coping with the long, dry season. During the rains, some ants are fed huge amounts of nectar by worker ants. These ants, known as honey pots, gradually swell up until they become too big to move. Then in the dry season, the honey pots become living larders, regurgitating the nectar to feed the rest of the colony.

The back part of this honey pot ant's body is filled with nectar. Honey pot ants can swell up to the size of a grape.

Shocking lizards

Frilled lizards spend most of their time in trees, where they can hide from predators, such as eagles. But if a predator gets too close, a lizard will open its mouth and suddenly stretch out the frill of skin around its neck like an umbrella. This makes it look much bigger and fiercer. The predator gets a shock, and the lizard is able to make its escape.

This frilled lizard is stretching its neck frill as far as it will go. When displaying, lizards' frills can be up to 35cm (14in) wide.

Rear view

By day, wombats shelter in underground burrows, which they dig with their strong front legs. Female wombats' pouches open backward, so their babies can peek out while they're digging, without getting a faceful of dirt.

This shows a baby wombat looking out of its mother's pouch.

The two holes on this platypus' beak are its nostrils, which it closes when underwater. You can also just make out one of its webbed feet, which help it to paddle through the water.

Southern forests

The forests of southern Australia and Tasmania are much cooler than the tropical forests of the north, and are made up mostly of eucalyptus trees. Many unique animals live there, including koalas, marsupial meat-eaters and an animal with the body of a mammal and a beak like a duck.

Pouched predators

Tasmanian devils are only the size of small dogs, but since marsupial wolves became extinct in the 1990s, they are now the largest marsupial meat-eaters. They prefer to scavenge food rather than hunt and have powerful jaws and teeth, which allow them to completely devour their prey – bones, fur and all.

A mother Tasmanian devil lies in her nest with her two babies. Tasmanian devils were named by early European settlers for their black coats and spine-chilling screeches.

Mixed-up animals

With their furry bodies, duck-like beaks and webbed feet, duckbilled platypuses look like lots of animals mixed together. On land, their sprawled legs give them a lizard-like walk, but they move quickly in water, where they hunt for food such as shrimp and snails. Males have poisonous spines on their back feet, which they can use to defend themselves against predators.

Born to climb

Although sometimes called koala bears, koalas aren't bears at all, but marsupials. They are excellent climbers, with two thumbs on each front paw for gripping onto branches, and ridged skin on their back feet to stop them from slipping. As they get both food and water from the eucalyptus leaves they eat, they need hardly ever come down to the ground.

This baby koala is about a year old. It can no longer fit in its mother's pouch, so it rides on her back instead. Soon, it will be strong enough to climb by itself.

A koala's two thumbs are on the opposite side of the hand to the fingers, giving a really strong grip.

★

Mimics

Lyrebirds are talented singers. When courting, males make an amazing array of sounds, mimicking other birds and even car engines and chainsaws, and adding these sounds to their songs. Males also fan out their tail feathers to attract females.

When a male lyrebird displays, his long tail feathers cascade over his head.

★

Internet link
For a link to a website where you can find out how a baby koala gets to its mother's pouch, go to
www.usborne-quicklinks.com

93

New Zealand

The isolated islands of New Zealand lie over 1,800km (1,120 miles) from the coast of Australia. Unlike anywhere else in the world, New Zealand has no native land mammals, with the exception of two species of bats. Its unusual wildlife includes flightless birds, giant insects and a reptile as old as the dinosaurs.

Grounded

Because there were no mammals to fear, some New Zealand birds adapted to living on the ground and, over time, lost the power of flight. New Zealand's flightless birds once ranged from giant birds larger than ostriches, to flightless parrots and ducks. But since people brought land mammals to New Zealand, many species have either died out, or are now very rare.

This is a takahe, a flightless bird believed to have died out in 1900, but rediscovered in 1948. There are only around 250 alive today.

Ancient scales

Tuataras look like large lizards, but are actually the only survivors of a group of reptiles from the age of the dinosaurs. They are now only found on a few small islands off the New Zealand coast. Tuataras grow very slowly. Their eggs take over a year to hatch and they don't reach their full size until they are about 20. However, they can live for over 70 years.

You can see this tuatara's scaly, loose skin, which is actually quite soft to touch.

This tui is hanging upside down so it can reach deep inside the flower for nectar.

Solo duets

Tuis are also known as New Zealand song birds because of their frequent singing. They actually have two voice boxes, so one bird can sing two songs at once. Each can be sung at a different pitch, as though the bird were doing a duet.

Internet link

For a link to a website where you can listen to tuis sing, go to www.usborne-quicklinks.com

Big eggs

Kiwis are flightless birds that grow to about the size of a hen. But the female's egg is six times as big as a hen's egg. The egg takes up so much space inside her body that she is unable to eat for three days before laying and can only waddle, with her legs wide apart. Once she lays her egg, the female leaves the male to look after it.

Egg inside kiwi

★

This picture shows how much space a kiwi's egg takes up inside her body.

Gentle giants

Giant wetas are among the heaviest insects, weighing three times as much as a mouse. They are a kind of cricket, but can't jump, because they are too heavy to leave the ground. Wetas can look fierce, as they throw their spiky legs in the air when threatened, but they rarely bite.

This giant weta has raised its back legs to scare off an attacker. They are not attractive insects – their name means "god of the ugly things" in Maori.

The Arctic

The Arctic is an ice-covered ocean surrounded by the northern edges of North America, Europe and Asia. The temperature in the Arctic hardly ever rises above freezing. In summer, the sun never sets and in winter, it is dark all the time. Only a very few animals stay in the Arctic all year round.

Internet link

For a link to a website where you can do an interactive quiz about Arctic animals, go to
www.usborne-quicklinks.com

ALASKA (USA)

Snowy owl

CANADA

Arctic tern

Narwhal whale

Lemming

RUSSIA

Killer whale

Stoat

Walrus

ARCTIC OCEAN

Snowshoe hare

Polar bears

Beluga whale

Arctic fox

GREENLAND (Denmark)

Caribou

Hooded seal

The Arctic region on this map is the area inside the dotted black line. Within the Arctic is Greenland, the world's largest island.

Map key

Forests

Tundra

Mountains

Ice & snow

This map shows just some of the animals that live in the Arctic.

Noisy animals

Walruses are the noisiest animals in the Arctic. On a calm day, their grunts and bellows can be heard many miles away. They spend most of their time in water, diving for shellfish, but come onto the ice to rest and to give birth to their young. They haul themselves out of the water using their incredibly strong tusks, which can be up to 90cm (3ft) long.

A walrus digs the tips of its tusks into the ice, so it can get a firm grip as it levers itself out of the water.

96

Microscopic life

Life in Arctic waters depends upon microscopic forms of life called phytoplankton that drift on the sea's surface. Phytoplankton convert the sun's energy into food. They are eaten by animal plankton, which in turn are eaten by fish, seals and even whales.

Big bears

Polar bears are the largest bears in the world. They live along the edge of the Arctic's floating sea ice, which they use as platforms to hunt for seals. They have to migrate hundreds of miles each year, following the ice as it extends far south in winter and retreats north in summer. They have large paws for their body size, which spread their weight as they move over ice and snow. Polar bears are also strong swimmers, often swimming up to 100km (60 miles) between patches of ice.

These polar bears are lying on the ice to rest. Although polar bears have white fur, their skin is black, as dark skin absorbs more heat than light skin. You can just see the dark skin showing through on their faces.

Inflatable heads

Some of the most bizarre-looking seals in the Arctic are hooded seals, so called because the males can inflate the tops of their heads into a kind of hood. They can also blow out the red skin inside their noses, either to warn off other males or to attract females during the breeding season. Males draw attention to their inflated noses by nodding their heads up and down to make their noses wobble.

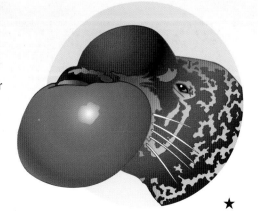

Male hooded seals inflate their noses like this by closing one nostril and blowing air through the other one.

★

Tundra and taiga

South of the Arctic Ocean lies a windswept stretch of land known as tundra. It is too cold for trees to grow there and the soil stays frozen all year round. South of the tundra lies the taiga, the largest band of forest in the world, home to bears, deer and countless small mammals and birds.

Surviving winter

Most animals leave the tundra during winter. The ones that remain are extremely hardy. Mice and lemmings keep warm by spending the winter in burrows under the snow, feeding on hay and seeds they have collected over the summer. Snowshoe hares spend the winter above ground. Their thick fur keeps them warm – it covers their entire bodies, even the gaps between their toes. They search for food on well-established trails, which become deeply worn in the snow.

This snowshoe hare's large back feet help to keep it from sinking into the snow.

This is a herd of male wapiti on the edge of the taiga. They have long, spindly legs to help them trek through the deep snow.

Chewing antlers

Many deer species, including moose, caribou and wapiti, live in the taiga. In winter, when food is scarce, they survive by eating bark and twigs. Then, late in winter, they shed their antlers. Deer sometimes chew on their old antlers to gain the extra minerals their bodies need.

Internet link

For a link to a website with a short video about life on the Arctic tundra, go to **www.usborne-quicklinks.com**

The Arctic fox's white winter coat makes it hard to see against the snow.

Changing coats

Tundra predators have to work hard to get their food. In winter, Arctic foxes follow polar bears to scavenge the remains of their kills, while stoats track prey by their scent over great distances. Both animals can change their coats to match the seasons, which helps to camouflage them as they hunt.

A stoat's coat during the summer

A stoat's coat during the winter

Antarctica

Antarctica is the world's coldest and emptiest continent. Few plants grow there and the largest land animal is a midge. The Southern Ocean, by contrast, thrives with life. Its waters are filled with plankton, fish, seals, whales and penguins.

Internet link

For a link to a website where you can play a game delivering animals to the North or South Pole, go to **www.usborne-quicklinks.com**

Plentiful penguins

Seven penguin species live in Antarctica. They all have short, tightly-packed feathers and a thick layer of fat to help them cope with the cold. Penguins can't fly, but they are fantastic swimmers. They use their stiff narrow wings as flippers in the water.

This is a map of Antarctica. The continent is permanently covered in a thick sheet of ice, which spreads out over nearby seas as well. In some places, the ice is over 3km (2 miles) deep.

Enormous mouthfuls

Thousands of whales arrive in Antarctica each summer to feed on the plankton. The largest are baleen whales. Instead of teeth, they have large bristles in their mouths, called baleen plates, which they use to filter food from the water. The plates enable the world's largest animals to feed on some of the smallest.

Map key

■ Mountains
□ Ice & snow

This map shows just some of the animals that live in the Antarctic.

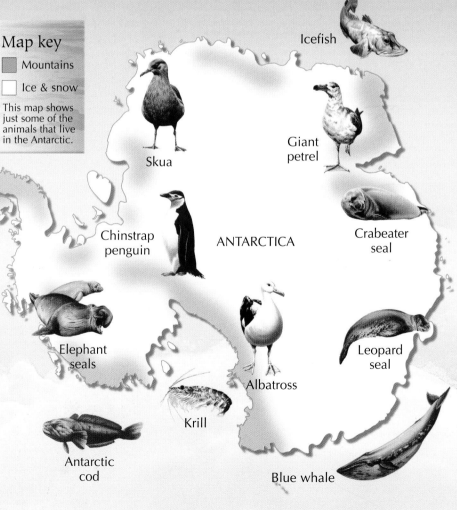

Icefish

Skua

Giant petrel

Chinstrap penguin

ANTARCTICA

Crabeater seal

Elephant seals

Albatross

Leopard seal

Krill

Antarctic cod

Blue whale

A baleen whale swims along with its mouth open, filling it with water and food.

Then it shuts its mouth, forcing the water out through its plates and trapping the food inside.

These Adélie penguins have come onto land to breed. Penguins find it hard to move on land and have a waddling walk. When going down slopes, they sometimes flop onto their bellies and slide down the ice.

Antifreeze fish

Many species of Antarctic fish, such as icefish and Antarctic cod, have developed an antifreeze chemical in their blood to help them survive in such cold waters. The antifreeze circulates around their bodies and stops ice crystals from forming. Without it, the fish would be frozen solid.

Killer seals

Vast colonies of seals live along the Antarctic coast. Leopard seals are the most ferocious, and are the only seals to feed on other seal species, although their main prey are Adélie penguins. Antarctica is also home to elephant seals – the world's largest seals. Males can weigh up to 5 tonnes (5.5 tons), which is heavier than a car.

This male elephant seal has opened its mouth to roar. Elephant seals get their name from the males' huge, trunk-like noses.

Ocean life

Earth is a watery world, with oceans covering more than two-thirds of its surface. The number and variety of creatures that live in the oceans is overwhelming. Most live near the sunlit surface, and in waters near the coast, but there is life even at the very bottom of the ocean.

This humpback whale uses its long flippers for turning and steering. Humpback whales have longer flippers than any other animal.

Little and large

There are more than 20,000 species of fish in the world, from tiny dwarf gobies, which are no bigger than the tip of your finger, to whale sharks, which grow longer than buses. All fish breathe by extracting oxygen from the water using their gills.

To breathe, a fish opens its mouth and takes in water. It extracts oxygen from the water as it passes over its gills.

Gills

It then pumps the water out through its gill slits.

★

Deadly species

Some of the world's most poisonous animals live in the oceans. Some, such as sea slugs, use poison to defend themselves against predators, while others use poison to hunt for prey. Jellyfish have stinging cells in their tentacles, which paralyze or kill their prey so they can eat them.

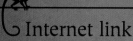

Internet link

For links to websites where you can listen to whale sounds and play underwater games, go to **www.usborne-quicklinks.com**

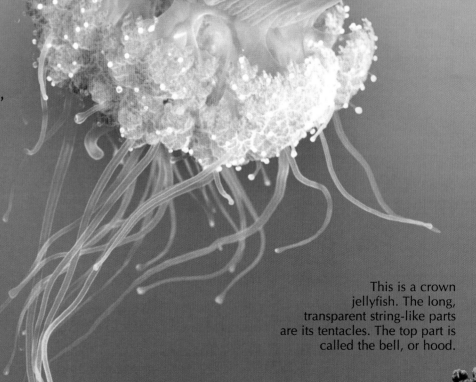

This is a crown jellyfish. The long, transparent string-like parts are its tentacles. The top part is called the bell, or hood.

Underwater giants

Whales are the biggest animals in the world.
Although they look like fish, they are actually
mammals. Whales can feed and breed underwater,
but still need to come to the surface to breathe.
Their breathing holes, known as blowholes, are on the
tops of their heads. This means they can breathe without
raising their heads far above the surface.

Turtle power

Turtles are reptiles that first took to the seas
over 200 million years ago. They are superbly
adapted for life in the ocean, with strong
front flippers and smaller back flippers
for steering. Their light, low-domed
shells enable them to slip easily
through water. When active, turtles
need to swim to the surface every
few minutes to breathe, but can
remain underwater for up to
two hours when resting.

These are Hawaiian green sea turtles.
They are named for the green fat
under their skin, which they get from
feeding on green algae.

Coral reefs

More than a quarter of all the creatures in the ocean live on coral reefs. The reefs are scattered throughout Earth's shallow, sunlit tropical waters. They provide food and shelter for a huge array of animals.

This is a day octopus, so called because it is most active during the day. Its eight arms are covered in suction cups for grasping its prey.

Hard and soft

There are two types of coral polyps – hard and soft. Soft corals have skeletons inside their bodies, whereas hard corals have solid skeletons outside their bodies. Hard coral polyps keep their tentacles inside their skeletons by day, but bring them out at night.

Nooks and crannies

Coral reefs are full of nooks and crannies where animals can hide and make their homes. Octopuses may seem too big to hide in reefs, but they are able to squeeze their soft, boneless bodies into amazingly small spaces.

This is a coral reef in the South Pacific. The bright corals are soft corals. The duller ones are hard corals. The photograph was taken during the day, so all you can see of the hard corals are their skeletons.

The yellow fish are anthias. They live on the reef in large numbers and feed on tiny animal plankton.

Cleaning fish

Fish need to keep clean, but cannot clean themselves. On coral reefs, small fish called cleaner wrasse pick off and eat the dead skin and pests on larger fish. Cleaner wrasse attract other fish to them by performing a zig-zagging dance. Banded coral shrimps also clean other animals, using their long, sharp claws to pick pieces of food out of their teeth.

★ A grouper will let cleaner wrasse into its mouth to clean its teeth without eating them.

★ Banded shrimps work together, feeding on fungus in a moray eel's teeth and skin.

This lionfish is covered in spines, but only the ones along its back are poisonous.

Poisonous spines

Many coral reef fish are highly territorial and fiercely guard the patch of the reef where they feed. Lionfish, for example, defend their territories by swimming up to invaders and pointing their poisonous spines at them. If the invader fails to retreat, the lionfish lunges forward to impale the invader on its spines.

The open ocean

Life in the open ocean is tough. There is nowhere to hide from predators, so most small fish live in huge groups, or schools, for protection. Predators often have to travel vast distances to find food, so they need to be fast and efficient hunters to survive.

Fast sharks

Most sharks in the open ocean are built for speed, with powerful tails, long slender bodies and pointed snouts for cutting through water. Larger sharks, such as oceanic whitetips, are slower and stockier, but are still capable of making sudden, lightning-speed charges after prey.

Surface breathers

There are over 20 dolphin species living in the open ocean. Dolphins are mammals and breathe air through blowholes on the tops of their heads. The most dangerous time in a dolphin's life is at birth, as a baby, or calf, needs to reach the surface quickly to take its first breath.

★

A mother dolphin gives birth near the surface, so the calf does not have far to go to take its first breath.

Using her head and snout, the mother lifts the calf above the water so it can breathe.

Oceanic whitetips are known for their large fins, which you can see clearly here. The tips of the fins are white, which is how the shark gets its name.

Internet link

For a link to a website where you can listen to dolphins and watch a short video clip, go to **www.usborne-quicklinks.com**

The whitetip won't eat these pilot fish, as it prefers larger, meatier prey. As well as eating the whitetip's leftover food, the pilot fish are using the shark as protection against other predators.

Flat bodies

Rays are close relatives of sharks. They have incredibly flat bodies and large, triangular fins. The largest are manta rays, which are wider than four cars parked next to each other. Manta rays feed on plankton, using lobes on their heads to guide the plankton into their mouths.

Manta rays swim by moving their fins up and down, like enormous wings.

Speedy swords

Billfish are among the fastest hunters in the ocean. They hunt in groups, swimming around schools of fish and using their long, sword-like bills to force them into tightly packed balls. Each billfish then takes a turn swimming through the ball, eating as many fish as it can.

As a billfish swims through a fish ball, it uses its sharp bill to stun or kill fish before snapping them up.

Deep sea monsters

The deep sea is home to some of the strangest creatures on Earth. There are no plants, so all the animals that live there are predators. They either prey on each other or eat the remains of other sea creatures that drift down from the waters above.

Spikes and mucus

Vampire squids live as deep down as 1,000m (3,280ft). They have sharp spikes covering the undersides of their tentacles. Folded back, these tentacles form a spiky shield to ward off predators. Vampire squid can also ooze a glowing mucus from the tips of their tentacles to surprise their attackers, giving them a chance to flee.

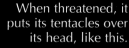

A vampire squid usually swims with its tentacles n front of its body.

When threatened, it puts its tentacles over its head, like this.

Internet link
For a link to a website where you can go on a virtual exploration of the bottom of the ocean, go to **www.usborne-quicklinks.com**

Fishing rods

Anglerfish have their very own "fishing rods" attached to their heads. Light-producing bacteria collect on the tips of the rods. When a hungry anglerfish wiggles the rod other fish swim up to it and the anglerfish gobbles them up.

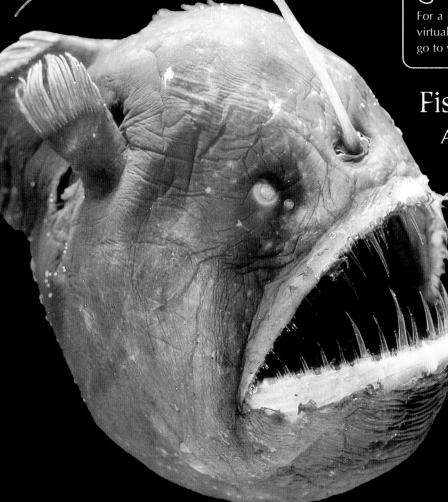

This is a female anglerfish. Females are only about the size of a baby's fist, but they are still bigger than males.

The gulper eel is not much more than a set of huge jaws attached to a very long stomach and a whip-like tail. Adult gulper eels reach lengths of over 1.8m (6ft). They mostly eat small fish and shrimp, but are able to unhinge their enormous jaws and stretch their stomachs to eat fish as big as themselves.

You can see this gulper eel's tiny eye at the tip of its snout (on the right). It doesn't rely on eyesight to catch prey, but swims along with its huge jaws wide open.

Avoiding enemies

With so many hungry predators around, deep-sea fish need cunning strategies for survival. Flashlight fish have pouches of light-producing bacteria to help them see and catch prey, but if they are spotted by predators, they can move a flap of muscle over the pouch to make themselves suddenly invisible.

Hatchet fish use the light-producing bacteria on their bodies to blend in with the water. They also have flattened bodies and silver sides that reflect any light, making them almost invisible to other fish.

★ A hatchet fish's lights are all along its belly.

★ Flashlight fish have a luminous pouch under each eye.

You can see this hatchet fish's flat, silvery body. Its mouth is upturned for scooping up prey.

Fact file
glossary and index

Animal facts

Animals are able to do many amazing and surprising things. Sometimes, we can only guess why they behave the way they do. Read on to find out some fascinating facts.

Arctic terns travel an incredible distance when they migrate. Each year, they fly from the Arctic to the Antarctic and back again. A one-way trip takes about two months.

When an assassin bug catches another bug to eat, it stabs the bug with its spiky mouth and injects it with a poison that dissolves the bug's insides. It then sucks these up, leaving behind a hollow shell.

Most predators only eat prey they have killed themselves. Grass snakes avoid being killed by pretending to be dead when a predator is nearby. They lie with their heads upside down and their tongues hanging out.

The front horn of a white rhinoceros can grow up to 1.5m (5ft) long. It is made of keratin – the same substance as our toenails.

Male seahorses are one of the few male animals to give birth to young. A female lays her eggs in a pouch on the male's tummy. After two weeks, he gives birth to tiny baby seahorses.

A camel can store up to 35kg (75lb) of fat in its hump. It can live off this fat, enabling it to go for up to 33 days without food.

King cobras have more venom than any other snake. One bite contains enough venom to kill a person in half an hour.

If a horned lizard is being attacked, it squirts large quantities of blood from small holes near its eyes. The blood tastes so bad that predators soon leave it alone.

Hermit crabs live inside other animals' old shells, as their own shells are too soft to protect them. They carry the shells on their backs and hide in them when threatened.

Young caddisflies have soft bodies. For protection, they produce a glue-like substance and make a case for themselves out of pebbles and shells.

These are spotted dolphins. Like all dolphins, they never go completely to sleep, but sleep by "switching off" half of the brain at a time. They need to keep the other half switched on to breathe.

These are macaws, a type of parrot. Parrots live longer than other birds – often for 50 years or more.

Canadian porcupines have about 30,000 quills, each up to 13cm (5in) long. Put end to end, the quills of one porcupine would reach a third of the way up Mount Everest.

Fleas can jump 200 times the length of their bodies. That's the same as you jumping about 240m (800ft). This is the actual size of a flea:

Hoatzins are also known as "stinkbirds" because they smell like cow dung. This is because of the way they digest their food.

When a rubber boa is threatened, it hides its head under its body and raises its head-like tail. If the enemy attacks, it will go for the boa's tail rather than its head.

Chamois, a type of mountain goat, are the fastest climbers. They can climb 915m (3,000ft) in only 15 minutes.

Freshwater hatchet fish can fly up to 3m (10ft) through the air. They fly by leaping out of the water, then flapping their fins.

Narwhals only have two teeth. The males' second tooth grows into a spiral tusk, which can be up to 2.5m (8ft) long.

Vampire bats drink around 70% of their body weight in blood every night. They get this blood from sleeping animals.

Dung beetles gather dung from other animals and make it into balls. Then they roll the dung into their burrows underground and lay their eggs in it.

Garden eels look as if they grow out of the seabed, but they actually live in holes in the sand. They poke out their heads to catch food that drifts by.

To hide from enemies, spittle bugs blow air and spit out of their bottoms, surrounding themselves in foam.

Internet link

For a link to a website with more amazing animal facts and stunning photographs, go to **www.usborne-quicklinks.com**

Animal records

Here are some spectacular animal records, including the biggest, smallest and fastest creatures alive today.

Internet link
For a link to a website where you can find out more amazing animal records, go to **www.usborne-quicklinks.com**

This enormous animal is an adult African elephant. These elephants are so huge they have to eat around 230kg (500lbs) of leaves a day.

Biggest

🦴 Animal – a fully-grown blue whale is as long as three buses and weighs more than 20 elephants.

🦴 Land animal – African elephants grow up to 4m (13ft) tall. Even newborn elephants are 1m (3ft) tall.

🦴 Birds – ostriches can be as tall as 2.5m (8ft).

🦴 Insects – American hercules beetles are one of the biggest insects, growing up to 19cm (7.5in) long.

Smallest

🦴 Animal – paramecium are the smallest animals. They can only be seen through a microscope.

🦴 Birds – hummingbirds are the smallest bird species in the world. The smallest is the size of a bee.

🦴 Mammals – Savi's pygmy shrews are the smallest mammals. They are about the size of your finger.

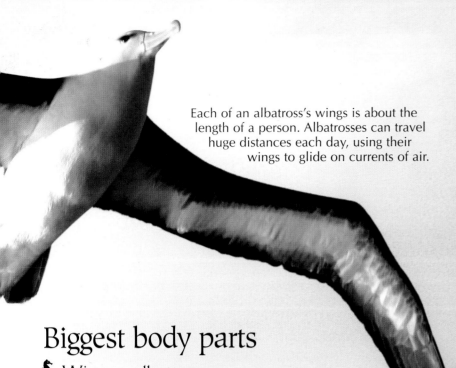

Each of an albatross's wings is about the length of a person. Albatrosses can travel huge distances each day, using their wings to glide on currents of air.

Deadliest

- Poison – box jellyfish are so poisonous that a single sting can kill a person within a few minutes.

- Bite – great white sharks have rows of sharp, saw-edged teeth up to 7.5cm (3in) long. They attack by taking one deadly, massive bite.

Biggest body parts

- Wings – albatrosses have the largest wingspan, measuring up to 3.5m (11ft) from tip to tip.

- Eyes – each of a giant squid's eyes is about the size of a person's head.

- Neck – a giraffe's neck is about 1.8m (6ft) – the same height as a tall man.

- Head – a sperm whale's head is about the same size as a car.

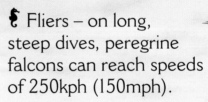

Fastest

- Swimmers – sailfish can reach speeds of up to 110kph (70mph).

- Fliers – on long, steep dives, peregrine falcons can reach speeds of 250kph (150mph).

- Runners – over short distances, cheetahs can run at 105kph (65mph), which is about the same speed as a fast car.

This cheetah is drawing its legs in, ready to spring forward again by pushing off with its back legs.

Animal quiz

How much do you know about animals? Test your knowledge with these quiz questions. The answers are on page 121.

Picture round

Look at the animal pictures on this page and see if you can answer the questions below.

1. This spider monkey has a prehensile tail, which means it can use its tail like an extra limb, to grip onto branches. Which continent is it from?

a) South America   b) Africa   c) Europe

2. The boxes below show close-ups of four different types of animals that appear in this book. Can you guess what they are?

If you look closely at this picture, you'll see that the spider monkey is grasping the branch with three legs and its tail.

a)   b)   c)   d)

3. The animals on the left are a mother and baby kangaroo. When the baby was born it was so small it could fit into a teaspoon, and it stayed in a pouch on its mother's tummy until it was about three months old. What kind of animal is a kangaroo?

a) an amphibian
b) a marsupial
c) a monotreme

This baby kangaroo, or joey, is learning to hop. It is around six months old.

Faking it

Could you make another animal believe you were one of its kind? Take this test to find out.

1. You are a blue-footed booby and want to attract a mate. What do you do?

a) make loud squawking noises
b) flap your wings
c) wave your feet around

2. You are a chimpanzee living in a group with other chimpanzees. How do you greet a friend coming up to you?

a) hold out your hand
b) give your friend a hard stare
c) scratch under your armpits

3. You are a male rhinoceros hornbill. Your mate has laid her eggs in a nest in a tree. What do you do next?

a) just fly away
b) sit on the eggs to help keep them warm
c) use pieces of mud to block your mate into the nest

4. You are an aye-aye and have spotted some delicious insects inside a tree. How do you get at them?

a) suck them out
b) tear through the bark to reach them
c) winkle them out with your fingers

Quick quiz

1. What are the only mammals that can fly?

2. Name the largest animal in the world.

3. How do you tell an alligator and a crocodile apart?

4. Why don't vultures have long feathers on their heads?

5. Can takahes fly?

6. What kind of monkey has the largest nose?

7. How do archer fish catch their prey?

8. Do penguins live in the Arctic or the Antarctic?

Internet link

For a link to a website with lots of interactive animal quizzes, go to **www.usborne-quicklinks.com**

This is a saltwater crocodile, from Australia. Saltwater crocodiles are the largest living reptiles, growing up to 7m (23ft) long.

Glossary

This glossary explains some of the words you may come across while reading about animals. Words in italics have their own entries elsewhere in the glossary.

adaptation The way a plant or animal *species* changes over time to suit its *habitat*.

amphibian A *cold-blooded* animal with soft skin. Most amphibians live on land but breed in water.

antenna One of a pair of thin projections on the heads of some insects and sea creatures, used for smelling, tasting and feeling.

antler One of a pair of structures on the heads of deer, used mainly for fighting. Usually only males have antlers. Antlers are made of bone and are shed and regrown each year.

arthropod An animal with a hard outer skeleton and jointed legs. Arthropods do not have backbones. Insects, spiders, centipedes, millipedes and crabs are all arthropods.

bacterium (pl. bacteria) A simple, single-celled organism found in the soil, in the air, and in plants and animals.

baleen plates Large bristles that hang down from the upper jaws of baleen whales. They are used to filter food from the sea.

binocular vision The ability to see objects using both eyes at the same time.

bird of prey A bird that hunts and eats other animals. Birds of prey are also known as raptors.

blowhole The breathing hole on the top of a whale or dolphin's head.

breeding Mating to produce young.

camouflage Body markings and coloration that make an animal blend in with its surroundings.

canopy The top layer of a forest, formed out of leaves and branches.

captive breeding Breeding *endangered species* in zoos or *nature reserves* to try to prevent them from becoming extinct.

carcass The body of a dead animal.

carnivore An animal that eats only meat.

cold-blooded Not being able to create heat inside the body. Cold-blooded animals take on the temperature of their surroundings.

colony A large group of animals living together.

compound eye An eye made up of many light-sensitive units.

conservation Protecting plants and animals and their habitats.

coral reef A structure made up of the skeletons of tiny animals called coral polyps.

courtship display A performance designed to attract a mate.

decomposer An organism that breaks down dead plants and animals and returns minerals to the soil.

delta A fan-shaped system of streams made by a river splitting up as it nears the sea.

den The home or shelter of a wild animal, especially of a meat-eating *mammal*.

desert A region that has little or no rain and where only a few plants or animals live.

display fighting Pushing or wrestling to show off strength. Display fighting is usually done by male animals to win the right to mate with a female. The fights rarely end in serious injury.

domesticated animal An animal that has been tamed and bred by people so that it can be used for food, clothing or transportation.

ecosystem A community of different types of animals and plants living together.

egg tooth The bump on a baby bird's beak that it uses to break out of its shell.

endangered species A *species* that is threatened by *extinction*.

environment Everything that makes up our surroundings, including the landscape, living things and the atmosphere.

extinction The death of an entire animal or plant *species*.

flock A group of one kind of animal that lives and feeds together, especially sheep, goats and birds.

food chain A series of living things, each one eaten by the next in line. For example, a plant is eaten by a *herbivore*, which is in turn eaten by a *carnivore*.

gill The organ with which most fish absorb oxygen from water.

grassland An open space where grasses grow and there are not many trees.

great ape Any of several *species* of apes with no tails, grasping hands and feet, and almost hairless faces. There are four kinds of great apes: gorillas, bonobos, orangutans and chimpanzees.

grooming The action of an animal cleaning another animal to remove parasites and dry skin. Grooming is also a sign of affection and strengthens the bonds between animals.

habitat The particular place where a plant or animal lives.

hatchling A newly hatched animal.

herbivore An animal that eats only plants.

hibernation A sleep-like state that some animals enter in order to survive cold, difficult conditions.

hive The home of a *colony* of bees, made out of thousands of wax cells.

Jacobson's organ An organ in the roof of an animal's mouth, used for detecting smells and tastes.

jet propulsion The action of an animal moving through water by taking water into its body and pushing it out again. Jellyfish, octopuses and squid use jet propulsion.

keratin The substance that makes up horns, hair and finger and toenails.

lodge A beaver's home, made out of sticks and mud. Beavers build lodges in the middle of ponds and the entrances are underwater.

mammal A *warm-blooded* animal that feeds its young with milk from its *mammary glands*. Mammals are usually covered with hair or fur. Most mammals give birth to live young, but *monotremes* lay eggs.

mammary gland Part of a *mammal's* body that makes milk.

mangrove swamp An area of coastline made up of the tangled roots of mangrove trees, mud flats and shallow water.

marsupial A type of *mammal* that gives birth to poorly-formed young. A baby marsupial completes its development in a pouch on its mother's tummy.

migration The movement of animals from one place to another at certain times of the year, to look for food or to find warmer surroundings.

mimicry The act of imitating dangerous animals to scare off *predators*.

monotreme An egg-laying *mammal*. There are only three kinds of monotremes, and they are found only in Australia and New Guinea.

national park An area of land protected by law from building and development.

nature reserve An area of land managed for the *conservation* of animals, plants and their habitats.

nectar The sweet juice produced by flowers.

nocturnal Active at night.

ocean One of the five large masses of salt water that cover the Earth's surface.

outback Dry, dusty area in central Australia.

pheromone A chemical released by certain animals to communicate with each other.

phytoplankton Plant *plankton*.

plankton Small plants or animals that drift in seas and lakes. Plankton is the main food source for many fish and whales.

plumage A bird's feathers.

pollen Tiny grains produced by plants, containing their male reproductive cells.

pollination The process of transferring *pollen* from one plant to the female reproductive organs of another plant of the same *species*, and fertilizing it so it can make seeds. Pollen can be carried from plant to plant by wind, water, or animals.

prairie Natural *grassland* in the USA.

predator An animal that hunts other animals for food.

prehensile Adapted for grasping. For example, many monkeys have prehensile tails which help them climb.

prey An animal that is hunted for food.

pride A group of lions who live together.

pup A term used for some baby animals, including dogs, seals, armadillos and beavers.

pupa Hard outer skin that grows around a caterpillar as it turns into a butterfly.

pupil The opening in the middle of an animal's eye that lets in light.

rainforest An area of dense, lush tropical forest, where a large amount of rain falls each year.

reptile A *cold-blooded* animal with scaly skin.

rodent A type of *mammal* that has front teeth especially adapted for gnawing. Mice and rats, for example, are rodents.

scavenger An animal that feeds on dead animals.

school A huge group of fish.

scute A scale or a plate made out of bone or *keratin*. Snakes, crocodiles and armadillos, for example, are covered in scutes.

social animal An animal that lives with other members of its *species* in highly structured groups.

spawn Eggs of animals that live in water, such as fish and frogs.

species A type of animal or plant.

steppe Natural *grassland* in eastern Europe and central Asia.

taiga A nearly continuous belt of evergreen forest that stretches across Asia, North America and Europe, close to the Arctic.

talon A claw, especially of a *bird of prey*. Talons are long, curved and sharp.

tentacle A long, thin body part used for feeding and grasping prey.

territory The area that an animal defends against intruders, especially of the same *species*.

thermal dance Hopping movements made by animals such as lizards and chameleons, so that no part of the body has to stay too long on hot ground.

threat display Activities to scare away another animal, usually of the same *species*, without actually fighting.

tundra The land bordering the Arctic, where a layer of the ground is permanently frozen and no trees grow.

waggle dance Movements made by honeybees to let other bees know where to find food.

warm-blooded Having a body that is able to produce its own heat. Animals that are warm-blooded can keep warm even if their surroundings are cold.

whiskers Any of the long, stiff hairs on a mammal's face, which respond to touch and help it to detect faint movements in the air.

Answers to animal quiz (pages 116–117)

Picture round

1. a. South America
2. a. zebra
   b. blue-ringed octopus
   c. cheetah
   d. okapi
3. b. a marsupial

Faking it

1. c. wave your feet around
2. a. hold out your hand
3. c. use pieces of mud to block your mate into the nest
4. c. winkle them out with your fingers

Quick quiz

1. Bats
2. Blue whale
3. The fourth tooth in the lower jaw of a crocodile can always be seen, even when it shuts its mouth.
4. So they can put their heads deep into carcasses to feed, without getting sticky feathers.
5. No
6. Proboscis monkey
7. By shooting jets of water out of their mouths, to knock insects off plants and into the water.
8. The Antarctic

Index

The numbers shown in *italics* refer to the animals on the maps.

A

Managing editor: Gillian Doherty. Managing designer: Mary Cartwright.
Senior designer: Stephen Moncrieff. Cartographer: Craig Asquith.
Additional illustrations: Craig Austin, Reuben Barrance, Verinder Bhachu, Richard Cox, Denise Finney,
David Hancock, Rebecca Hardy, Philip Hood, Steven Kirk, Stephen Lings, Rachel Lockwood,
Malcolm McGregor, Maurice Pledger, Chris Shields, Candice Whatmore, John Woodcock, David Wright.

First published in 2005 by Usborne Publishing Ltd, 83-85 Saffron Hill, London EC1N 8RT, England.
www.usborne.com Copyright © 2005 Usborne Publishing Ltd. The name Usborne and the devices ♀ ⊕ are Trade
Marks of Usborne Publishing Ltd. All rights reserved. No part of this publication may be reproduced, stored in a
retrieval system, or transmitted in any form or by any means, electronic, mechanical, photocopying, recording or
otherwise, without the prior permission of the publisher. UE. First published in America in 2005. Printed in Dubai.

Usborne Publishing is not responsible and does not accept liability for the availability or content of any website
other than its own, or for any exposure to harmful, offensive, or inaccurate material which may appear on the Web.
Usborne Publishing will have no liability for any damage or loss caused by viruses that may be downloaded as a
result of browsing sites it recommends. The downloadable pictures in this book are the copyright of
Usborne Publishing and may not be used for any commercial or profit-related purpose.

Acknowledgements

Every effort has been made to trace the copyright holders of the material in this book. If any rights have been omitted, the publishers offer to rectify this in any subsequent editions following notification. The publishers are grateful to the following organizations and individuals for their permission to reproduce material (t=top, m=middle, b=bottom, l=left, r=right):

Cover: (tl) © Ralph Henning/Alamy, (b) © Amos Nachoum/Image Bank/Getty Images, (tr) © ANDY HARMER/SCIENCE PHOTO LIBRARY, (spine) © Digital Vision, (back cover) © Digital Vision; **Endpapers** © Digital Vision; **p1** © SteveBloom.com; **p2** © SteveBloom.com, (background) © Digital Vision; **p4** (tl) © Niall Benvie/CORBIS; **p5** © Doug Perrine/Seapics.com; **p6** © Joseph Van Os/Image Bank/Getty Images; **p6-7** © Tim Davis/CORBIS; **p7** © NHPA/Stephen Dalton; **p8** © Steve Bloom Images/Alamy; **p9** (t) © Hamman, David/Animals Animals/Earth Scenes, (b) © Warren Photographic; **p10** (tr) NHPA/Stephen Dalton; **p10-11** © M. Iwago/Minden/FLPA; **p11** © Jany Sauvanet/Still Pictures; **p12** © SteveBloom.com; **p13** (tl) © Warren Photographic, (b) © Bob Elsdale/Image Bank/Getty Images; **p14** (bl) © Nat Sumanatemeya/Seapics.com, (tr) © Karen Gowlett-Holmes/OSF/Photolibrary.com; **p15** (t) © John Brown/OSF/Photolibrary.com, (b) © DIGITAL VISION LIMITED/Powerstock; **p16** (b) © Dr. M.S. Mayilvahnan, (t) © NHPA/Stephen Dalton; **p16-17** © Franco/Bonnard/Still Pictures; **p18** © Frans Lanting/Minden/FLPA; **p19** (t) © NHPA/Daniel Heuclin, (b) © PREMAPHOTOS/Naturepl.com; **p20** © Tui De Roy/Minden/FLPA; **p21** (t) © Joe McDonald/CORBIS, (b) © Karl Ammann/CORBIS; **p22** © Tim Davis/CORBIS; **p23** (t) © Warren Photographic, (b) © M & C Denis-Huot/Still Pictures; **p24** © James D. Watt/Seapics.com; **p25** (t) © SteveBloom.com, (b) © Paul Horsted/Alamy; **p26** (b) © Mark Conlin/Seapics.com; **p26** (m) © Digital Vision; **p26-27** (t) © Lynda Richardson/CORBIS; **p27** © Warren Photographic; **p28** (b) © Michael & Patricia Fogden/Minden/FLPA, (t) © Michael & Patricia Fogden/CORBIS; **p29** © Anthony Bannister, Gallo Images/CORBIS; **p30** © Kennan Ward/CORBIS; **p30-31** (t) © Royalty Free/CORBIS; **p31** © Ken Preston-Mafham/Premaphotos Wildlife; **p32** © Dave Watts/Naturepl.com; **p32-33** © Doug Perrine/Seapics.com; **p33** (br) © NHPA/Martin Harvey; **p34** © Michael & Patricia Fogden/Minden/FLPA, © Buddy Mays/CORBIS; **p35** © Paul Sterry/Alamy; **p36** (b) © Powerstock; **p36-37** (t) © Tui De Roy/Minden/FLPA; **p37** © Tui De Roy/Minden/FLPA; **p38** © Theo Allofs/CORBIS; **p39** © Michael & Patricia Fogden/CORBIS, (b) © Mitsuhiko Imamori/Minden/FLPA; **p40** © Malie Rich-Griffith/Alamy; **p41** (b) © Theo Allofs/CORBIS, (t) © Roy Toft/National Geographic Image Collection; **p42** © Genevieve Vallee/Alamy; **p43** © Peter Oxford/Naturepl.com; **p44** © Steve Satushek/Image Bank/Getty Images; **p45** (l) © NHPA/Stephen Dalton, (r) © W. Perry Conway/CORBIS; **p46** (b) © W. E. Garrett/National Geographic Image Collection, (t) © Joe McDonald/CORBIS; **p47** © TeamHusar.com; **p48** © franzfoto.com/Alamy, (background) © Jim Brandenburg/Minden/FLPA; **p49** © Jeff Vanuga/CORBIS; **p50** © Terry W. Eggers/CORBIS; **p50-51** © Arizona Art Wolfe/Stone/Getty Images; **p51** © Tim Flach/Stone/Getty Images; **p52-53** © Masa Ushioda/Alamy; **p53** © Stan Osolinski/OSF/Photolibrary.com; **p54** © M. Watson/ardea.com; **p55** © Frans Lanting/Minden/FLPA; **p56** © fogdenphotos.com; **p56-57** © Michele Westmorland/CORBIS; **p57** © zefa/F. Lemmens; **p58** © Martin Harvey/Alamy; **p59** (b) © Anup Shah/Naturepl.com, (t) © Martin Harvey/CORBIS; **p60-61** © SteveBloom.com; **p61** (t) © Beverly Joubert/National Geographic Image Collection; **p62** © SteveBloom.com; **p62-63** (t) © Peter Johnson/CORBIS; **p63** (b) © Tony Heald/Naturepl.com; **p64** (l) © Nick Garbutt/Naturepl.com, (br) © Chris Hellier/CORBIS; **p65** © SteveBloom.com; **p66** © Tom Brakefield/CORBIS; **p67** © Bildagentur Franz Waldhaeusl/Alamy; **p68** © Konrad Wothe/Minden/FLPA; **p69** (t) © Gallo Images/CORBIS, (b) © Dave Watts/Naturepl.com; **p70** © Jose B. Ruiz/Naturepl.com; **p71** (b) © Powerstock, (t) © M. Watson/ardea.com; **p72** © Brian J. Skerry/National Geographic Image Collection; **p73** (t) © Laurie Campbell/RSPB Images, (b) © Bryn Colton/Assignments Photographers/CORBIS; **p74** (t) © Photowood Inc./Alamy, (b) © Anup Shah/Naturepl.com; **p75** © David Kjaer/Naturepl.com; **p76** © Steve Kaufman/CORBIS; **p76-77** © Felicity Volk/Lonely Planet Images; **p77** (t) © Steve Kaufman/CORBIS, (b) © Mark Yates/Naturepl.com; **p78** © Kenneth Fink/ardea.com; **p78-79** (t) © StockConnection/Alamy; **p79** © ImageState/Alamy; **p80** © TeamHusar.com; **p81** (b) © Heather Angel/Natural Visions, (t) © Powerstock; **p82** © Timothy Laman/National Geographic/Getty Images; **p82-83** (b) © Warren Photographic; **p83** © Frans Lanting/Minden/FLPA; **p84** © Photodisc Green/Getty Images; **p85** © Tom Brakefield/CORBIS; **p86** © Jean-Paul Ferrero/Auscape International; **p87** © Doug Perrine/Seapics.com; **p88** © Phil Savoie/Naturepl.com; **p89** © Anup Shah/Naturepl.com; **p90** © Dave Watts/Naturepl.com; **p91** (t) © NHPA/ANT Photo Library, (b) © Jean Paul Ferrero/ardea.com; **p92** (t) © Nicole Duplaix/National Geographic/Getty Images, (b) © Dave Watts/ANTPhoto.com.au; **p93** © KLEIN/Still Pictures; **p94** (t) © John Cancalosi/Naturepl.com, (b) © Rob Suisted/www.naturespic.com; **p95** (t) © Geoff Moon/Natural Visions, (b) © Rob Suisted/www.naturespic.com; **p96-97** © SteveBloom.com; **p98** © Tom Brakefield/CORBIS; **p98-99** (t) © Thomas Mangelsen/Minden/FLPA; **p99** © Jim Zuckerman/CORBIS; **p100-101** (t) © Royalty Free/CORBIS; **p101** © Richard Herrmann; **p102** (br) © Reinhard Dirscherl/Alamy; **p102-103** © NHPA/ANT Photo Library; **p103** (b) © David B. Fleetham/Seapics.com; **p104** © Brandon Cole Marine Photography/Alamy; **p104-105** (b) © Mark Conlin/Seapics.com; **p105** (t) © Maximilian Weinzierl/Alamy; **p106-107** © David Shen/Seapics.com; **p108** © Norbert Wu/Norbert Wu Productions; **p108-109** © Doc White/Seapics.com; **p109** (r) © Paulo De Oliveira/OSF/Photolibrary.com; **p110-111** © SteveBloom.com; **p112** (b) © Digital Vision; **p112-113** (background) © SteveBloom.com; **p113** © SteveBloom.com; **p114** © NATURAL SELECTION INC./Bruce Coleman; **p114-115** (t) © Norma Joseph/Alamy; **p115** (b) © Andy Rouse/The Image Bank/Getty Images; **p116** (t) © ART WOLFE/SCIENCE PHOTO LIBRARY, (b) © Ruoso Cyril/Still Pictures; **p117** © Tobias Bernhard/Image Bank/Getty Images.